W9-BGN-475

Marijuana

Other Books of Related Interest:

Opposing Viewpoints Series

Medical Marijuana

At Issue Series

Are Americans Overmedicated?

Current Controversies Series

Medical Marijuana

"Congress shall make
no law . . . abridging
the freedom of speech,
or of the press."

First Amendment to the US Constitution

The basic foundation of our democracy is the First Amendment guarantee of freedom of expression. The Opposing Viewpoints series is dedicated to the concept of this basic freedom and the idea that it is more important to practice it than to enshrine it.

OPPOSING
VIEWPOINTS®
SERIES

Marijuana

Noah Berlatsky, Book Editor

GREENHAVEN PRESS
A part of Gale, Cengage Learning

GALE
CENGAGE Learning®

Detroit • New York • San Francisco • New Haven, Conn • Waterville, Maine • London

GALE
CENGAGE Learning·

Elizabeth Des Chenes, *Managing Editor*

© 2012 Greenhaven Press, a part of Gale, Cengage Learning.

Gale and Greenhaven Press are registered trademarks used herein under license.

For more information, contact:
Greenhaven Press
27500 Drake Rd.
Farmington Hills, MI 48331-3535
Or you can visit our Internet site at gale.cengage.com

For product information and technology assistance, contact us at

Gale Customer Support, 1-800-877-4253
For permission to use material from this text or product, submit all requests online at www.cengage.com/permissions

Further permissions questions can be emailed to permissionrequest@cengage.com

Articles in Greenhaven Press anthologies are often edited for length to meet page require-ments. In addition, original titles of these works are changed to clearly present the main thesis and to explicitly indicate the author's opinion. Every effort is made to ensure that Greenhaven Press accurately reflects the original intent of the authors. Every effort has been made to trace the owners of copyrighted material.

Cover Image copyright © pashabo/Shutterstock.com.

LIBRARY OF CONGRESS CATALOGING-IN-PUBLICATION DATA

Marijuana / Noah Berlatsky, book editor.
    p. cm. -- (Opposing viewpoints)
    Includes bibliographical references and index.
    ISBN 978-0-7377-5733-0 (hardcover) -- ISBN 978-0-7377-5734-7 (pbk.)
    1. Marijuana abuse--United States. 2. Marijuana--Physiological effect. 3. Marijuana--Therapeutic use. 4. Drug legalization--United States. 5. Drug control--United States. I. Berlatsky, Noah.
    HV5825.M3427 2012
    362.29'50973--dc23
                                                                2011042809

Printed in the United States of America
1 2 3 4 5 6 7 16 15 14 13 12

Contents

Chapter 3: Should Medical Marijuana Be Legalized?

Why Consider Opposing Viewpoints?

> *"The only way in which a human being can make some approach to knowing the whole of a subject is by hearing what can be said about it by persons of every variety of opinion and studying all modes in which it can be looked at by every character of mind. No wise man ever acquired his wisdom in any mode but this."*
>
> *John Stuart Mill*

In our media-intensive culture it is not difficult to find differing opinions. Thousands of newspapers and magazines and dozens of radio and television talk shows resound with differing points of view. The difficulty lies in deciding which opinion to agree with and which "experts" seem the most credible. The more inundated we become with differing opinions and claims, the more essential it is to hone critical reading and thinking skills to evaluate these ideas. Opposing Viewpoints books address this problem directly by presenting stimulating debates that can be used to enhance and teach these skills. The varied opinions contained in each book examine many different aspects of a single issue. While examining these conveniently edited opposing views, readers can develop critical thinking skills such as the ability to compare and contrast authors' credibility, facts, argumentation styles, use of persuasive techniques, and other stylistic tools. In short, the Opposing Viewpoints Series is an ideal way to attain the higher-level thinking and reading skills so essential in a culture of diverse and contradictory opinions.

In addition to providing a tool for critical thinking, Opposing Viewpoints books challenge readers to question their own strongly held opinions and assumptions. Most people form their opinions on the basis of upbringing, peer pressure, and personal, cultural, or professional bias. By reading carefully balanced opposing views, readers must directly confront new ideas as well as the opinions of those with whom they disagree. This is not to argue simplistically that everyone who reads opposing views will—or should—change his or her opinion. Instead, the series enhances readers' understanding of their own views by encouraging confrontation with opposing ideas. Careful examination of others' views can lead to the readers' understanding of the logical inconsistencies in their own opinions, perspective on why they hold an opinion, and the consideration of the possibility that their opinion requires further evaluation.

Evaluating Other Opinions

To ensure that this type of examination occurs, Opposing Viewpoints books present all types of opinions. Prominent spokespeople on different sides of each issue as well as well-known professionals from many disciplines challenge the reader. An additional goal of the series is to provide a forum for other, less known, or even unpopular viewpoints. The opinion of an ordinary person who has had to make the decision to cut off life support from a terminally ill relative, for example, may be just as valuable and provide just as much insight as a medical ethicist's professional opinion. The editors have two additional purposes in including these less known views. One, the editors encourage readers to respect others' opinions—even when not enhanced by professional credibility. It is only by reading or listening to and objectively evaluating others' ideas that one can determine whether they are worthy of consideration. Two, the inclusion of such viewpoints encourages the important critical thinking skill of objectively evaluating an author's credentials and bias. This evaluation will illuminate an author's reasons for taking a particular stance on an issue and will aid in readers' evaluation of the author's ideas.

It is our hope that these books will give readers a deeper understanding of the issues debated and an appreciation of the complexity of even seemingly simple issues when good and honest people disagree. This awareness is particularly important in a democratic society such as ours in which people enter into public debate to determine the common good. Those with whom one disagrees should not be regarded as enemies but rather as people whose views deserve careful examination and may shed light on one's own.

Thomas Jefferson once said that "difference of opinion leads to inquiry, and inquiry to truth." Jefferson, a broadly educated man, argued that "if a nation expects to be ignorant and free ... it expects what never was and never will be." As individuals and as a nation, it is imperative that we consider the opinions of others and examine them with skill and discernment. The Opposing Viewpoints series is intended to help readers achieve this goal.

David L. Bender and Bruno Leone,
Founders

Introduction

"The underlying ethos of Canada's drug policy has been the promotion of public health, even when this meant tolerating modest levels of illicit drug abuse."

—David Anderson et al.,
The Khat Controversy:
Stimulating the Debate on Drugs,
New York: Berg, 2007.

In the United States, marijuana use is prohibited by the federal government, but some states allow limited use of the substance for medical reasons. Canada has also had conflicts surrounding marijuana legislation, and as of 2012 the legality of marijuana in Canada is under serious dispute.

Marijuana was first banned in Canada in 1923 by the Opium and Drugs Act. In modern times, however, this ban has faced a number of legal challenges, particularly for medical use of marijuana. In 2000 the Ontario Court of Appeal voided a federal law prohibiting the possession of less than thirty grams of marijuana. The grounds for striking down the law were that it violated the Canadian Charter of Rights and Freedoms, the Canadian bill of rights.

A year after this case, in 2001, Canada legalized medical marijuana. Patients could be prescribed medical marijuana for a number of conditions, including pain or nausea associated with multiple sclerosis, spinal cord injury, or cancer, or for other conditions subject to the determination of a specialist. Health Canada, the Canadian department of health, stated on its website that medical marijuana legislation did not mean that all marijuana was legal. It emphasized, "Marihuana is categorized as a controlled substance. It is not legal to grow or possess marihuana except with legal permission by Health Canada."

In April 2011, however, an Ontario court declared that the government's efforts to distinguish between medical marijuana and general use were unacceptable. "Justice Donald Taliano found that the vast majority of doctors refuse to prescribe the drug. Patients are therefore forced to break the law, either by growing their own or buying it on the black market," according to an April 19, 2011, article on the GlobalPost website. In his ruling the judge said, "Seriously ill persons who need marihuana to treat their symptoms are forced to choose between their health and their liberty."

Commentators differed on the justice of the ruling. According to an April 13, 2011, editorial in the *Globe and Mail*, "The constitutional issue is easy to understand. The state's marijuana ban aims to protect people from harm, yet the ban imposes harm on sick people." The *Globe and Mail* also argued that the ruling should be used as the springboard for a debate about the decriminalization of marijuana, wondering "where is the high degree of harm, to others or self, that requires criminal sanction [for marijuana possession], including jail?"

The *National Post*, on the other hand, agreed that Canada should decriminalize marijuana but argued that such changes should be made through Parliament, not through the courts: "As was the case with same-sex marriage, such seismic shifts in Canada's traditional moral code garner more public support, more quickly, when made by Canadians' elected representatives rather than by appointed judges," the editorial board said in an April 18, 2011, article.

In his ruling, Justice Taliano gave the government ninety days to fix the medical marijuana laws. If it failed to do so, marijuana would effectively be legalized in Ontario. However, the Conservative government of Prime Minister Stephen Harper was committed to a get-tough-on-crime position and appealed the court ruling. Before the ninety days could run out, the appeals court suspended the lower court decision pending a review of the case. Alan Young, the lawyer for the defendant, noted that a failure of the appeal could have serious consequences for the government. Quoted in an April 13, 2011, article in the *Toronto Star*, Young said, "If the government is not successful on appeal, they are going to be caught between a rock and a hard place because they don't have an alternative program in mind. They don't have a plan B. They're in trouble."

The controversy over marijuana use in Canada reflects public opinion. A March 18, 2010, article on the CBC News website noted that half of Canadians surveyed believe that possession of small amounts of marijuana for personal use should not be classified as a crime, while half believe it should. Canadians are thus split evenly over the issue of whether to legalize marijuana. However, the article observes that Canadian opinion seems to be shifting in favor of legalization; in 2000 only 45 percent supported decriminalizing marijuana.

The legalization of marijuana is but one of the many controversial issues explored in the following chapters of *Opposing Viewpoints: Marijuana*: Is Marijuana Harmful?, Are There Medical Benefits to Using Marijuana?, Should Medical Marijuana Be Legalized?, and Should Recreational Marijuana Be Legalized? The authors present different views on both the dangers and benefits of marijuana and the consequences of legalization.

OPPOSING
VIEWPOINTS®
SERIES

CHAPTER 1

Is Marijuana Harmful?

Chapter Preface

According to a number of studies, marijuana may be linked to increased risks of heart attack and stroke. For example, a study conducted by Murray Mittleman, associate professor of medicine at Harvard Medical School, concluded that smoking marijuana increased the heart rate by approximately forty beats per minute and also increased blood pressure, according to a March 3, 2000, article by Holcomb B. Noble in the *New York Times*. As a result, "A middle-age person's risk of heart attack rises nearly fivefold in the first hour after smoking marijuana."

Similarly, in their book *Marijuana Medical Handbook: Practical Guide to the Therapeutic Uses of Marijuana*, Dale Gieringer, Ed Rosenthal, and Gregory T. Carter note, "Right after smoking, THC [tetrahydrocannabinol, the main active ingredient in marijuana] speeds up the heart by as much as 30 to 60 beats per minute." The authors suggest that this may be a problem for those with heart disease and add that "some heart patients experience chest pains or other circulatory discomfort when they smoke marijuana." However, the authors argue, "There is no reason to think it is dangerous for persons in normal health [to experience this level of accelerated heart rate], any more than the fast heartbeat caused by jogging or by a game of tennis."

Another study found that smoking marijuana results in increased production of a protein that raises the body's levels of blood fats associated with heart attack and stroke, according to Ed Edelson in a May 13, 2008, article in *U.S. News & World Report*. Government researchers, therefore, concluded that marijuana might be a factor in heart disease. However, Christopher Granger, a Duke University professor quoted in the same article, said that while the study was interesting, it did not prove that a cause-and-effect relationship exists between smoking marijuana and increased risk of heart disease.

Some studies have found that chemicals in marijuana may be beneficial for the heart. According to a study by Michael Roth, a professor at the University of California, Los Angeles medical school, small amounts of THC may help fight atherosclerosis. Roth did note that marijuana smoking can have adverse effects on the heart as well. To gain the heart benefits of THC, it might be necessary to develop prescription drugs, "rather than using marijuana or oral THC as medicines," Roth stated in an April 6, 2005, article on *WebMD*.

This chapter examines other possible harmful effects of marijuana, such as addiction, lung cancer, and interference with sexual functioning.

> *"All of the studies clearly show the earlier someone starts taking marijuana, the greater their vulnerability to addiction disorders and psychiatric disorders."*

Marijuana Is Addictive and Is Linked to Use of Harder Drugs

Rita Rubin

Rita Rubin writes on medical topics for USA Today. *In the following viewpoint, she says that marijuana can result in addiction, including withdrawal symptoms. She notes that while the exact relationship between marijuana use and use of harder drugs is not clear, the evidence does show that many people who use marijuana go on to use cocaine, heroin, and other substances. She says that marijuana use is associated with lower quality of life, and she reports on marijuana users who wish they had not started using the drug.*

As you read, consider the following questions:

1. Why does Rubin say it is impossible to determine whether marijuana is a gateway drug?

2. What percentages of eighth graders and twelfth graders said they used marijuana in 2006 and in 1991, according to Rubin?

3. How does Harrison Pope define heavy marijuana users?

Tyreol Gardner first smoked marijuana when he was 13.

"The main reason I tried it was curiosity," Gardner recalls. "I wanted to see what it felt like."

Hard to Quit

He liked what it felt like, and by age 15, he was smoking pot every week. He supported his habit with the money his parents gave him for getting straight A's on his report card. They didn't have a clue.

"By 16, when I got my license, it turned into a fairly everyday thing," says Gardner, now 24. "I believe it is very addictive, especially for people with addictive personalities."

Millions of baby boomers might disagree. After all, they smoked marijuana—the country's most popular illicit drug—in their youth and quit with little effort.

But studies have shown that when regular pot smokers quit, they do experience withdrawal symptoms, a characteristic used to predict addictiveness. Most users of more addictive drugs, such as cocaine or heroin, started with marijuana, scientists say, and the earlier they started, the greater their risk of becoming addicted.

Many studies have documented a link between smoking marijuana and the later use of "harder" drugs such as heroin and cocaine, but that doesn't necessarily mean marijuana causes addiction to harder drugs.

"Is marijuana a gateway drug? That question has been debated since the time I was in college in the 1960s and is still being debated today," says Harvard University psychiatrist Harrison Pope, director of the Biological Psychiatry Laboratory at Boston's McLean Hospital. "There's just no way scientifically to end that argument one way or the other."

That's because it's impossible to separate marijuana from the environment in which it is smoked, short of randomly assigning people to either smoke pot or abstain—a trial that would be grossly unethical to conduct.

More Likely to Use Other Drugs

"I would bet you that people who start smoking marijuana earlier are more likely to get into using other drugs," Pope says. Perhaps people who are predisposed to using a variety of drugs start smoking marijuana earlier than others do, he says.

Besides alcohol, often the first drug adolescents abuse, marijuana may simply be the most accessible and least scary choice for a novice susceptible to drug addiction, says Virginia Tech psychologist Bob Stephens.

No matter which side you take in the debate over whether marijuana is a "gateway" to other illicit drugs, you can't argue with "indisputable data" showing that smoking pot affects neuropsychological functioning, such as hand-eye coordination, reaction time and memory, says H. Westley Clark, director of the Center for Substance Abuse Treatment at the Substance Abuse and Mental Health Services Administration.

Adolescents have the greatest rates of marijuana use, and they also have the greatest amount to lose by using marijuana, scientists say.

"Adolescence is about risk-taking, experimentation," says Yasmin Hurd, professor of psychiatry, pharmacology and biological chemistry at the Mount Sinai School of Medicine in New York who last summer published a rat study that found early exposure to THC, the psychoactive ingredient in marijuana, led to a greater sensitivity to heroin in adulthood.

"All of the studies clearly show the earlier someone starts taking marijuana, the greater their vulnerability to addiction disorders and psychiatric disorders. I'm so shocked still that so many parents are not considering enough the dangers of early drug use."

Marijuana use by adolescents in the USA declined slightly from 2005 to 2006, but it's still more common than it was 15 years ago, according to "Monitoring the Future," an ongoing study by the University of Michigan that tracks people from the eighth grade through young adulthood. It's paid for by the National Institute on Drug Abuse, or NIDA, part of the National Institutes of Health.

In 2006, 11.7% of eighth graders said they had used marijuana during the past year, compared with 6.2% of eighth graders in 1991. Among 12th graders [in 2006], 31.5% said they had used marijuana in the previous year; in 1991, 23.9% said they had.

"You are at school, and your main job as an adolescent is to learn and memorize," NIDA director Nora Volkow says. But if you keep becoming intoxicated by smoking marijuana, she says, you'll fall further and further behind in your studies. "How are you going to catch up?"

In a study comparing heavy marijuana users with people who'd had minimal exposure to the drug, Pope found that the former had lower verbal IQ scores than the latter. In a 2003 paper, he and his co-authors postulated three potential reasons: innate differences between the groups in cognitive ability that predated first marijuana use, an actual toxic effect of marijuana on the developing brain or poorer learning of conventional cognitive skills by young marijuana users who skipped school.

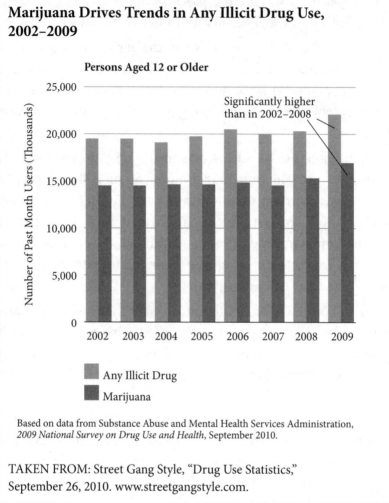

Marijuana Drives Trends in Any Illicit Drug Use, 2002–2009

Persons Aged 12 or Older

Significantly higher than in 2002–2008

Based on data from Substance Abuse and Mental Health Services Administration, *2009 National Survey on Drug Use and Health*, September 2010.

TAKEN FROM: Street Gang Style, "Drug Use Statistics," September 26, 2010. www.streetgangstyle.com.

Skipping School

By the time Gardner was a junior, he started skipping high school regularly to smoke pot. "I would always find somebody who wasn't at school that day and get high with them," he says. Gardner says he missed 50 days in the first semester of his senior year. His parents discovered his stash of marijuana and sent him to a psychiatrist.

His grades plummeted; his college plans evaporated.

When he was 16 or 17, Gardner says, he was charged at least twice with possession of marijuana and underage possession of alcohol. The court sent him to a three-month outpatient treatment program. He attended weekly sessions and underwent urine checks.

But it didn't stick. He celebrated the end of the program by getting high on pot and alcohol. By 18, "I was pretty heavy into cocaine," Gardner says. Crystal meth and intravenous heroin followed.

"I was always looking for the ultimate high. It was like a constant search, and I never found it. . . . By the end, it was a living hell for me."

Finally, Gardner says, his parents persuaded him to enter an inpatient treatment program in Winchester, Va. They spoke from experience. When he was 8, Gardner says, his father stopped using drugs while in prison for possession. "My mom got clean while he was in prison."

Gardner says he has been off drugs and alcohol for 14 months. He works in a Winchester factory that makes patio decking. He graduated high school because a teacher took pity on him and let him try to make up the work he had missed. More than six years after graduating, Gardner hopes to go to college to study psychology.

Research shows marijuana users are significantly less satisfied with the quality of their lives than nonusers, a revelation "as telling as any very fancy story of molecules," Volkow says.

Yet, she says, "I think there is a general sense that marijuana is a relatively benign drug and does not produce addiction." Although over the past decade, "research clearly has provided unequivocal evidence that . . . some people can become addicted to marijuana."

Stephens has conducted seven large treatment studies of marijuana dependence, or addiction. "There's never any shortage of people who meet this definition," says Stephens, who edited the 2006 book *Cannabis Dependence*.

Pot Is Addictive

Pope has studied heavy marijuana users, whom he defines as having smoked pot at least 5,000 times, or once a day for nearly 14 years. On average, his subjects, ages 30 to 55, reported having smoked marijuana 20,000 times.

Pope required the volunteers to abstain from smoking pot for 28 days and used urine samples for confirmation.

"We had them rate various symptoms on a day-by-day basis," he says. "We were able to show there is a clear withdrawal syndrome."

His research found the most common symptom of marijuana withdrawal was irritability, followed by trouble sleeping and loss of appetite. Symptoms began to subside after a week and disappeared by the end of two weeks.

"We've had some people in our study who reported quite a lot of craving. They were quite miserable not being allowed to smoke marijuana," Pope says, although "certainly, one does not see craving even remotely to the degree you would . . . with heroin or alcohol or cocaine."

Marijuana today is more potent and therefore more toxic than marijuana grown in the 1970s, Volkow says. Back then, she says, plants typically contained only 2% THC. Today, she says, marijuana plants typically contain 15% THC.

Even if today's marijuana is more potent, Stephens says, he's not convinced that makes a difference.

"The evidence of its increased potency is overrated," he says. Samples of marijuana grown in the 1970s might have appeared to be less potent than they actually were because they weren't fresh when tested. And, Stephens speculates, marijuana users might just smoke more of less-potent pot, and vice versa.

Rachel Kinsey says drug addiction runs in her mother's family, although not in her immediate family. Kinsey, 24, started drinking alcohol at 14 and smoking marijuana at 15—

"definitely a predecessor for everything else I used." She began using Ecstasy and cocaine at 17, then heroin at 18.

"I did graduate high school, and I went off to college, but I withdrew after a month," says Kinsey, of Richmond, Va. She used the diagnosis of mononucleosis she'd received the week before college as an excuse.

"I don't think I was ready for the responsibility, and I wanted to continue to use while I was in college. I was at the point where I just didn't care about college. I was already using heroin."

She moved in with her boyfriend and his father, both of whom used heroin. At 19, she got pregnant. She moved back in with her mother, substituted methadone for heroin and gave the baby up for adoption. Practically as soon as she delivered, she was back to using heroin.

About five months after her son was born in May 2003, Kinsey entered inpatient addiction treatment. During the 30-day program, she became involved with a man who went back to using cocaine after ending treatment. Kinsey says she didn't want to go back to using cocaine or heroin, "but for some reason I thought it was OK to drink and go back to smoking weed."

When she turned 21 in fall 2003, "it was off to the races. For some reason, I felt (turning 21) gave me the right to drink if I wanted to."

From January to August 2004, Kinsey says, she was charged three times with driving under the influence of alcohol and marijuana.

With the help of another stay at a treatment center, Kinsey hasn't used drugs or alcohol since Aug. 25, 2004, the day after her last DUI arrest. She's halfway toward graduating from nursing school and works as a nurse tech in a hospital. For the first time, she has signed a lease on an apartment and pays rent.

She can't drive until September 2008 and then only to work, to school and to 12-step meetings.

If she had to do it all over again, she says, she never would have started smoking marijuana.

"You never know where it's going to lead you," she says. "You don't know that you're not going to become an addict, so it's not worth the risk."

"*The data don't show that marijuana causes use of other drugs, but instead indicate that the same factors that make people likely to try marijuana also make them likely to try other substances.*"

Marijuana Is Not a Gateway Drug

Bruce Mirken

Bruce Mirken served as director of communications for the Marijuana Policy Project from 2001 to 2009. In the following viewpoint, he argues that marijuana is not a gateway drug that leads users to try more dangerous substances such as speed and heroin. He points to two recent studies, both of which found no link between marijuana and further drug use. Instead, he says, the studies showed that marijuana users share traits that may lead to other drug use.

As you read, consider the following questions:

1. According to Mirken, how does the gateway theory present drug use?

2. Who did the Brisbane study follow, according to Mirken?

3. What did the Brisbane authors mean when they said that the gateway effects were likely to be "social rather than pharmacological"?

Two recent studies should be the final nails in the coffin of the lie that has propelled some of this nation's most misguided policies: the claim that smoking marijuana somehow causes people to use hard drugs, often called the "gateway theory."

Bad to Worse

Such claims have been a staple of the White House Office of National Drug Control Policy under present drug czar John Walters. Typical is a 2004 New Mexico speech in which, according to the *Albuquerque Journal*, "Walters emphasized that marijuana is a 'gateway drug' that can lead to other chemical dependencies."

The gateway theory presents drug use as a tidy progression in which users move from legal drugs like alcohol and tobacco to marijuana, and from there to hard drugs like cocaine, heroin and methamphetamine. Thus, zealots like Walters warn, marijuana is bad because it leads to things that are even worse.

It's a neat theory, easy to sell. The problem is, scientists keep poking holes in it—the two new studies being ... just the most recent examples.

In one National Institute on Drug Abuse–funded study, researchers from the University of Pittsburgh tracked the drug use patterns of 224 boys, starting at age 10 to 12 and ending at age 22. Right from the beginning these kids confounded expectations. Some followed the traditional gateway paradigm, starting with tobacco or alcohol and moving on to marijuana, but some reversed the pattern, starting with marijuana first. And some never progressed from one substance to another at all.

When they looked at the detailed data on these kids, the researchers found that the gateway theory simply didn't hold; environmental factors such as neighborhood characteristics played a much larger role than which drug the boys happened to use first. "Abusable drugs," they wrote, "occupy neither a specific place in a hierarchy nor a discrete position in a temporal sequence."

Lead researcher Dr. Ralph E. Tarter told the *Pittsburgh Post-Gazette*, "It runs counter to about six decades of current drug policy in the country, where we believe that if we can't stop kids from using marijuana, then they're going to go on and become addicts to hard drugs."

Australian Study

Researchers in Brisbane, Australia, and St. Louis reached much the same conclusion in a larger and more complex study published last month [November 2006]. The research involved more than 4,000 Australian twins whose use of marijuana and other drugs was followed in detail from adolescence into adulthood.

Then—and here's the fascinating part—they matched the real-world data from the twins to mathematical models based on 13 different explanations of how use of marijuana and other illicit drugs might be related. These models ranged from pure chance—assuming that any overlap between use of marijuana and other drugs is random—to models in which underlying genetic or environmental factors lead to both marijuana and other drug use or models in which marijuana use causes use of other drugs or vice versa.

When they crunched the numbers, only one conclusion made sense: "Cannabis and other illicit drug use and misuse co-occur in the population due to common risk factors (correlated vulnerabilities) or a liability that is in part shared." Translated to plain English: The data don't show that marijuana causes use of other drugs, but instead indicate that the same factors that make people likely to try marijuana also make them likely to try other substances.

In the final blow to claims that marijuana must remain illegal to keep us from becoming a nation of hard-drug addicts, the researchers added that any gateway effect that does exist is "more likely to be social than pharmacological," occurring because marijuana "introduces users to a provider (peer or black marketeer) who eventually becomes the source for other illicit drugs." In other words, the gateway isn't marijuana; it's laws that put marijuana into the same criminal underground with speed and heroin.

The lie that marijuana somehow turns people into junkies is dead. Officials who insist on repeating it as a way of squelching discussion about commonsense reforms should be laughed off the stage.

| "The prudence principle should be sufficient to convince everybody that lung cancer has to be added to the list of secondary effects of cannabis smoking."

Marijuana Use Is Linked to Lung Cancer

Crystal Phend

Crystal Phend is a senior staff writer for MedPage Today. *In the following viewpoint, she discusses a study that indicates that a link exists between smoking marijuana and lung cancer. She notes that the study finds that a single marijuana joint may be as carcinogenic as twenty cigarettes. The study's authors urge doctors to ask patients about marijuana use. Phend notes that other experts say more studies may be needed.*

As you read, consider the following questions:

1. What was the increased risk of lung cancer for marijuana smokers who smoked one joint a day for ten years, according to the viewpoint?

2. According to Phend, what respiratory effects have been found with marijuana?

3. What percentage of lung cancer among those younger than twenty-five in New Zealand did the researchers attribute to cannabis smoking?

Smoking a single marijuana joint may be as carcinogenic to the lungs as 20 tobacco cigarettes, researchers here determined.

Cannabis and Carcinogens

Those who smoked the equivalent of one joint a day for 10 years had a 5.7 times higher lung cancer risk than nonsmokers even after adjusting for tobacco use, reported Richard Beasley, M.B.Ch.B., of the Medical Research Institute of New Zealand here, and colleagues in the Feb. 1 [2008] issue of the *European Respiratory Journal*.

The effect on lung cancer risk in the population-based case-control study was even greater than the one joint to five cigarettes equivalency for lung damage previously reported by the research group.

Smoke from cannabis contains up to twice as many carcinogenic polycyclic aromatic hydrocarbons and tends to be smoked without filters while inhaling more deeply, leading to higher concentrations of smoke inhaled, the investigators noted.

Although cough, wheeze, and other respiratory effects expected with any type of smoking have been found with marijuana, the association with lung cancer has been inconclusive.

However, the New Zealand findings provide sufficient evidence that some components of cannabis itself or cannabis smoke are real lung carcinogens, according to an accompanying editorial by Christian Brambilla, M.D., and Marc Colonna, Ph.D., both of the Institut Albert Bonniot in Grenoble, France.

"The prudence principle should be sufficient to convince everybody that lung cancer has to be added to the list of secondary effects of cannabis smoking, along with asthma and chronic obstructive pulmonary disease," they wrote.

Adverse Effects on the Lungs

Numerous studies have shown marijuana smoke to contain carcinogens and to be an irritant to the lungs. In fact, marijuana smoke contains 50–70 percent more carcinogenic hydrocarbons than tobacco smoke. Marijuana users usually inhale more deeply and hold their breath longer than tobacco smokers do, which further increase the lungs' exposure to carcinogenic smoke.

"NIDA InfoFacts: Marijuana,"
National Institute on Drug Abuse, November 2010.
http://drugabuse.gov.

Physicians should ask patients about smoking of both tobacco and cannabis in everyday practice, they said.

But Norman H. Edelman, M.D., chief medical officer of the American Lung Association, was more cautious.

"Since there are some studies that reach other conclusions, we can't say that it nails down [the risk]," he said. "We need larger studies."

Risk of Cancer

The researchers conducted in-home interviews on cancer risk factors including cannabis use among 79 lung cancer patients younger than 55 and 324 age-matched controls randomly selected from eight New Zealand health districts covering a population of 1.8 million.

Lung cancer patients were identified from hospital databases or the national cancer registers from 2001 through 2005. Most had non-small-cell lung cancer (80%) and none had lung metastasis from a distant primary.

The proportion of controls who had ever smoked cannabis was 36% after adjustment for the general population age distribution.

Overall, 26.6% of lung cancer patients in the study reported smoking at least 20 joints in their lifetime, whereas 12% of control participants had.

For every one joint-year—the equivalent of one joint per day for one year—smoked, the risk of lung cancer rose 8%.

The association between cannabis and lung cancer was strengthened with adjustment for the growth rate of lung cancer, by excluding exposure in the five years before baseline or diagnosis, "as would be expected if a causal association existed."

The association was similar to the 7% risk seen for each pack-year of tobacco smoking.

Participants who had smoked 20 or more joints over their lifetime were not at significantly higher risk than those who had smoked fewer.

Only those in the highest use group with more than 10.5 joint-years of exposure were at significantly elevated lung cancer risk compared with nonsmokers after adjustment for tobacco exposure, age, sex, ethnicity, and family history of lung cancer.

Further adjustment excluding exposure over the prior five years, which would not have been expected to have contributed to the current diagnosis, showed a similar pattern, with 5.2-fold higher risk for those in the highest exposure tertile.

But this is not likely a threshold effect, Dr. Beasley and colleagues said.

Rather, the lack of association at lower intake levels could have been the result of the relatively small number of marijuana users in the study and the young age of the participants "reducing the time available for high numbers of joint-years to accumulate."

Even using the prevalence of the highest tertile of cannabis smoking among the control group, the researchers estimated that about 5% of lung cancer among those younger than 55 in New Zealand may be attributable to cannabis smoking.

"If any increased risk was maintained as these young people age," they said, "then a considerable burden from lung cancer due to cannabis smoking may occur in the future."

Although they said participants were unaware during their interview that the study was focused on cannabis use, they noted that epidemiologic research on cannabis use has been fraught with difficulties.

"While it is important to interpret the findings in the context of these limitations," the investigators concluded, "the balance of evidence would suggest a positive association between cannabis and lung cancer."

| "The THC in cannabis seems to lessen the tumor-promoting properties of marijuana smoke."

Pot Smoking Not Linked to Lung Cancer

Salynn Boyles

Salynn Boyles is a reporter who covers medical issues for WebMD and other publications. In the following viewpoint, she writes that scientists in a recent study were surprised to discover no connection between smoking marijuana and cancer. The results are confusing, she says, because marijuana smoke is known to contain carcinogens and so should, in theory, cause an increased cancer risk. Researchers speculate that THC, a component of marijuana, may inhibit the formation of tumors, therefore off-setting the cancer-causing effects of marijuana smoke.

As you read, consider the following questions:

1. Why does Boyles say that the study was limited to people younger than sixty?

2. How many joints had the heaviest marijuana users in the study smoked, according to Boyles?

3. In what ways does Tashkin say that THC restricts tumor formation?

People who smoke marijuana do not appear to be at increased risk for developing lung cancer, new research suggests.

While a clear increase in cancer risk was seen among cigarette smokers in the study, no such association was seen for regular cannabis users.

Even very heavy, long-term marijuana users who had smoked more than 22,000 joints over a lifetime seemed to have no greater risk than infrequent marijuana users or nonusers.

The findings surprised the study's researchers, who expected to see an increase in cancer among people who smoked marijuana regularly in their youth.

"We know that there are as many or more carcinogens and co-carcinogens in marijuana smoke as in cigarettes," researcher Donald Tashkin, MD, of UCLA's David Geffen School of Medicine tells WebMD. "But we did not find any evidence for an increase in cancer risk for even heavy marijuana smoking." Carcinogens are substances that cause cancer.

Tashkin presented the findings today at the American Thoracic Society's 102nd international conference, held in San Diego.

Boomers Reaching Cancer Age

The study population was limited to people who were younger than 60 because people older than that would probably not have used marijuana in their teens and early adult years.

"People who may have smoked marijuana in their youth are just now getting to the age when cancers are being seen," Tashkin says.

A total of 611 lung cancer patients living in Los Angeles County, and 601 patients with other cancers of the head and neck were compared with 1,040 people without cancer matched for age, sex, and the neighborhood they lived in.

All the participants were asked about lifetime use of marijuana, tobacco, and alcohol, as well as other drugs, their diets, occupation, family history of lung cancer, and socioeconomic status.

The heaviest marijuana users in the study had smoked more than 22,000 joints, while moderately heavy smokers had smoked between 11,000 and 22,000 joints.

While two-pack-a-day or more cigarette smokers were found to have a 20-fold increase in lung cancer risk, no elevation in risk was seen for even the very heaviest marijuana smokers.

The more tobacco a person smoked, the greater their risk of developing lung cancer and other cancers of the head and neck. But people who smoked more marijuana were not at increased risk compared with people who smoked less and people who didn't smoke at all.

The THC Connection

Studies suggest that marijuana smoke contains 50% higher concentrations of chemicals linked to lung cancer than cigarette smoke. Marijuana smokers also tend to inhale deeper than cigarette smokers and hold the inhaled smoke in their lungs longer.

So why isn't smoking marijuana as dangerous as smoking cigarettes in terms of cancer risk?

The answer isn't clear, but the experts say it might have something to do with tetrahydrocannabinol, or THC, which is a chemical found in marijuana smoke.

Cellular studies and even some studies in animal models suggest that THC has antitumor properties, either by encouraging the death of genetically damaged cells that can become cancerous or by restricting the development of the blood supply that feeds tumors, Tashkin tells WebMD.

In a review of the research published last fall, University of Colorado molecular biologist Robert Melamede, PhD, concluded that the THC in cannabis seems to lessen the tumor-promoting properties of marijuana smoke.

The nicotine in tobacco has been shown to inhibit the destruction of cancer-causing cells, Melamede tells WebMD. THC does not appear to do this and may even do the opposite.

While there was a suggestion in the newly reported study that smoking marijuana is weakly protective against lung cancer, Tashkin says the very weak association was probably due to chance.

Cancer risk among cigarette smokers was not influenced by whether or not they also smoked marijuana.

"We saw no interaction between marijuana and tobacco, and we certainly would not recommend that people smoke marijuana to protect themselves against cancer," he says.

> "Given the high prevalence of cannabis use and the associations reported between frequent cannabis use and a range of sexual health issues, clinicians should routinely enquire about patients' cannabis use."

Marijuana Interferes With Sexual Functioning

Anthony M.A. Smith, Jason A. Ferris, Judy M. Simpson, Julia Shelley, Marian K. Pitts, and Juliet Richters

Anthony M.A. Smith, Jason A. Ferris, Judy M. Simpson, Julia Shelley, Marian K. Pitts, and Juliet Richters are all professors at institutions in Australia. In the following viewpoint, they report on a study of Australians that linked marijuana use with sexual problems in men and women. In particular, they found that marijuana use was associated with multiple sexual partners, an increased incidence of sexually transmitted diseases in women, and problems achieving orgasm in men. The authors conclude that there is evidence that marijuana is tied to sexual problems, and they recommend that doctors should routinely ask patients about marijuana use.

Anthony M.A. Smith, Jason A. Ferris, Judy M. Simpson, Julia Shelley, Marian K. Pitts and Juliet Richters, "Cannabis Use and Sexual Health," *The Journal of Sexual Medicine*, vol. 7, no. 2.1, February 2010, pp. 787–793. Copyright © 2010 by John Wiley & Sons, LTD. All rights reserved. Reproduced by permission of Blackwell Publishers, LTD.

As you read, consider the following questions:

1. What evidence do the authors provide that the public does not well understand risks associated with cannabis?

2. Where do the authors say they got the data for their study?

3. According to the authors, why might men be self-medicating with cannabis?

Cannabis is the most widely cultivated and used illicit drug with an estimated 147 million people or 2.5% of the world population using it annually [1]. Its use has been linked to earlier and more frequent sexual activity, having multiple sexual partners, having casual sexual partners while traveling, inconsistent contraceptive use, and being diagnosed with a sexually transmissible infection [2–7].

Uncertainty Around Marijuana and Sex

Despite the prevalence of cannabis use and its apparent association with adverse sexual health outcomes, the link between cannabis use and sexual health has been the subject of remarkably few population-based studies. Those studies that have been done have focused on adolescents and young adults [8–15]. It is a criminal offence to possess, cultivate or sell cannabis in all states of Australia. However, possessors of small amounts of cannabis for personal use are generally issued an infringement fine rather than being prosecuted. The person may also be required to attend a cannabis education session. One in three Australians has ever used cannabis [16], and in many social circles it is little stigmatized [17]. As it grows easily in Australian conditions, it can be obtained cheaply and without recourse to dealers of other illicit drugs, though many users do buy from dealers [18]. Its use widened from a small counterculture minority in the 1970s to broader but not completely mainstream social groups in the 2000s. Many of the correlations found between cannabis use (lifetime or recent) and health outcomes are related to socio-demographic factors or social location (rates of use are higher among gay men and lesbians [18, 20], prisoners [21], injecting drug users [18], and young people attending music festivals [19]), and to psychological factors among users such as risk-taking and psychological distress [16].

Public perception of the risks associated with cannabis use is not well understood. In one study, 27% of people aged 14 and older indicated that they were uncertain about whether there was any health problems associated with cannabis use. The health risks identified included respiratory problems, addiction and the escalation of drug use, and the risk of driving accidents [22]. Sexual health was not identified as being among the domains of cannabis-related health risk.

The present study examines the socio-demographic correlates of cannabis use in a large, population-based study of adults aged 16–64 years, and the relationship between the frequency of cannabis use and the number of sexual partners in the past year, condom use at the most recent sexual encounter, and the reporting of sexually transmissible infection and sexual difficulties.

Marijuana Linked to Sexual Problems

Data came from the 2005 intake interview of the Australian Longitudinal Study of Health and Relationships [23]. This is a computer-assisted telephone interview study of Australians aged 16–64 years.

The interview covered a broad range of socio-demographic and health topics with a focus on sexual and reproductive health issues. Cannabis use was assessed with three questions: whether the participant had used cannabis at least 10 times in their life; whether they had used it in the 12 months prior to interview; and if so, whether they had used it daily, weekly, or less often.

Study Data on the Demographics of Marijuana Use in Australia

Women's frequency of cannabis use

Age (4,299)	None %	Less than weekly %	Weekly %	Daily %
16–25 (721)	89.71	7.05	2.43	0.81
26–35 (829)	90.44	7.55	0.70	1.31
36–45 (1,068)	92.35	5.39	1.09	1.17
46–55 (1,050)	97.78	1.67	0.48	0.08
56–64 (631)	99.08	0.92	0.00	0.00

Men's frequency of cannabis use

Age (4,350)	None %	Less than weekly %	Weekly %	Daily %
16–25 (844)	84.19	9.39	3.36	3.06
26–35 (737)	80.88	13.01	3.73	2.38
36–45 (960)	86.36	9.30	1.48	2.87
46–55 (1,082)	93.60	3.47	1.08	1.85
56–64 (727)	97.94	0.80	0.57	0.69

TAKEN FROM: Anthony M.A. Smith et al., "Cannabis Use and Sexual Health," *Journal of Sexual Medicine*, February 2010.

Outcomes of interest were the number of sexual partners in the year prior to interview (none, one, two, or more), condom use at most recent vaginal intercourse (no, yes), or anal intercourse (no, yes; asked only of men who had reported having sex with other men), diagnosis with a sexually transmissible infection in the year prior to interview (no or yes to any of: chlamydia, syphilis, gonorrhea, and genital herpes), and the presence for 1 month or more of the following sexual problems: lacking interest in sex, inability to orgasm, reaching orgasm too quickly, reaching orgasm too slowly, experiencing pain during intercourse, not finding sex pleasurable, anxiety about one's ability to perform sexually, vaginal dryness (women), and trouble keeping an erection (men) [24]. Where a sexual problem was reported, the extent to which it was experienced as problematic was ascertained: not a problem, a minor problem, somewhat of a problem, or a major problem [25].

Socio-demographic factors controlled for included: age group (16–25, 26–35, 36–45, 46–55, 56–64), language spoken at home (English, other), sexual identity (heterosexual, homosexual, bisexual), educational attainment (lower secondary, secondary, postsecondary), occupation (professional, associate professional, trades, unskilled), and legal marital status (married, never married, separated, divorced, or widowed). All these factors have been identified as associated with one or more of the outcomes of interest, and analyses were conducted separately of men and women [26–30]. . . .

A total of 8,656 people completed the interview with an overall response rate of 56% [23]. Of the 8,650 who answered the questions about cannabis use, 754 (8.7%) reported cannabis use in the previous year with 126 (1.5%) reporting daily use, 126 (1.5%) reporting weekly use, and 502 (5.8%) reporting use less often than weekly. Cannabis use was more commonly reported by men than by women (11.2% vs. 6.1%), and in both men and women was more commonly reported by participants younger than 36 years. However, cannabis use was reported in all age groups with daily use reported by all age groups of men and all but the oldest age group among women. There was a strong association between frequency of cannabis use and frequency of tobacco use in both men and women. Among male daily cannabis users, 70% were daily tobacco users compared with 18% for male cannabis nonusers. Among female daily cannabis users, 69% were daily tobacco users compared with 18% for female cannabis nonusers. Cannabis use was also associated with a non-heterosexual identity, lower educational attainment, lower status occupation, and not being married.

The number of sexual partners in the year prior to interview was strongly associated with the frequency of cannabis use. Adjusted odds ratios (OR) [a statistical tool to determine probabilities] indicate that frequent cannabis use by women was associated with an increased likelihood of reporting more than two sexual partners and a markedly reduced likelihood of reporting no partners rather than one. Among men, the relationship between frequency of cannabis use and reporting no partners rather than one was less clear, although any cannabis use was associated with a doubling of the likelihood of reporting two or more partners in the previous year compared with one partner. Among both men and women, the adjusted OR indicated no association between frequency of cannabis use and the likelihood of condom use at their most recent intercourse. Frequency of cannabis use among men was not associated with reporting a diagnosis of a sexually transmissible infection in the previous year, but daily cannabis use among women was associated with a marked increase in the likelihood of reporting such a diagnosis.

Among women, there was no association between any of the sexual problems and frequency of cannabis use in the adjusted analyses. For men, however, there were significant associations between daily cannabis use and reporting an inability to reach orgasm, reaching orgasm too quickly, and reaching orgasm too slowly. Among the 144 men who reported an inability to orgasm, there was no association between frequency of cannabis use and the extent to which inability to orgasm was experienced as problematic. However, among the 424 men who reported reaching orgasm too quickly, there was an association between frequency of cannabis use and the extent to which reaching orgasm too quickly was experienced as problematic such that more frequent cannabis use was associated with experiencing reaching orgasm too quickly as more problematic.

Marijuana, Orgasm, Dysfunction, and STIs

Frequent cannabis use, particularly daily use, is associated with a range of health and behavioral outcomes. For example, frequent users are more likely than others to report two or more sexual partners in the previous year, as has been found in other studies [9].

Female daily cannabis users are significantly more likely than nonusers to report the diagnosis of a sexually transmissible infection in the previous year. Although frequent cannabis use appears unrelated to sexual problems in women, it clearly interferes with orgasm in men and its use is associated with the delay or prevention of orgasm in some men and with orgasm too soon in others. That there is an association between frequency of cannabis use and the extent to which reaching orgasm too quickly is problematic raises the possibility that men are self-medicating with cannabis to delay orgasm.

We failed to find any association between frequency of cannabis use and trouble keeping an erection. This is consistent with the finding of [researcher S.D.] Johnson and colleagues who also failed to find an association between lifetime cannabis use and "inhibited sexual excitement (i.e., lack of erection in men, lack of arousal for women)"[7]. However, there have been reports that very high doses of cannabis have been associated with an "inability to perform" [32], and that this may be related to changes in plasma testosterone such that modest doses increase plasma testosterone but that high doses lower testosterone below baseline [32].

Consistent with the present article, Johnson and colleagues found an association between cannabis use and inhibited orgasm, such that a history of cannabis use was associated with being more likely to report a recent history of an inability to orgasm [7]. [J] Halikas and colleagues also found that cannabis use was associated with an increased duration of intercourse and a decreased number of orgasms [33].

The present study has a number of strengths and weaknesses. Its strengths include the large sample, wide age range of participants, and high response rate. Weaknesses include a reliance on self-report and the attendant possibility of a social desirability bias [that is, respondents may change their answers so they will be viewed favorably].

Given the high prevalence of cannabis use and the associations reported between frequent cannabis use and a range of sexual health issues, clinicians should routinely enquire about patients' cannabis use and, if frequent use is reported, take a detailed sexual history and manage the patient accordingly.

These findings could also provide useful input to health promotion and/or health education campaigns aiming to reduce frequent cannabis use.

References

1. World Health Organization. *Cannabis (facts and figures)*. Geneva: WHO; 2008. Available at http://www.who.int/ substance_abuse/facts/cannabis/en/ (accessed December 16, 2008).

2. Abel EL. Marihuana and sex: a critical survey. *Drug Alcohol Depend* 1981; 8:1–22.

3. Arvidson M, Kallings I, Nilsson S, Hellberg D, Mårdh PA. Risky behavior in women with history of casual travel sex. *Sex Transm Dis* 1997; 24:418–21.

4. Boyer CB, Shafer MA, Teitle E, Wibbelsman CJ, Seeberg D, Schachter J. Sexually transmitted diseases in a health maintenance organization teen clinic: Associations of race, partner's age, and marijuana use. *Arch Pediatr Adolesc Med* 1999; 153:838–44.

5. Clark T, Robinson E, Crengle S, Watson P. Contraceptive use by Maori youth in New Zealand: Associated risk and protective factors. *N Z Med J* 2006; 119:U1816.

6. Guo J, Staton B, Cottrell L, Clemens RL, Li X, Harris C, Marshall S, Gibson C. Substance use among rural adolescent virgins as a predictor of sexual initiation. *J Adolesc Health* 2005; 37:252–5.

7. Johnson SD, Phelps DL, Cottler LB. The association of sexual dysfunction and substance use among a community epidemiological sample. *Arch Sex Behav* 2004; 33:55–63.

8. Bell R, Wechsler H, Johnston LD. Correlates of college marijuana use: Results of a US national survey. *Addiction* 1997; 92:571–81.

9. Brodbeck J, Matter M, Moggi F. Association between cannabis use and sexual risk behavior among young heterosexual adults. *AIDS Behav* 2006; 10:599–605.

10. Castilla J, Barrio G, Belza MJ, De La Fuente L. Drug and alcohol consumption and sexual risk behaviour among young adults: Results from a national survey. *Drug Alcohol Depend* 1999; 56:47–53.

11. Graves KL, Leigh BC. The relationship of substance use to sexual activity among young adults in the United States. *Fam Plann Perspect* 1995; 27:18–22, 33.

12. Lowry R, Holtzman D, Truman BI, Kann L, Collins JL, Kolbe LJ. Substance use and HIV-related sexual behaviours among US high school students: Are they related? *Am J Public Health* 1994; 84:1116–20.

13. Martino SC, Collins RL, Ellickson PL. Substance use and vulnerability to sexual and physical aggression: A longitudinal study of young adults. *Violence Vict* 2004; 19:521–40.

14. Mott FL, Haurin RJ. Linkages between sexual activity and alcohol and drug use among American adolescents. *Fam Plann Perspect* 1988; 20:128–36.

15. Roberts TA, Auinger P, Ryan SA. Body piercing and high-risk behavior in adolescents. *J Adolesc Health* 2004; 34:224–9.

16. Australian Institute of Health and Welfare. *2007 National drug strategy household survey: First results.* Canberra: AIHW; 2008.

17. Holt M. Young people and illicit drug use in Australia. *Social research issues paper No. 3.* Sydney: National Centre in HIV Social Research, University of New South Wales; 2005.

18. Black E, Roxburgh A, Degenhardt L, Bruno R, Campbell G, De Graaff B, Fetherston J, Kinner S, Moon C, Quinn B, Richardson M, Sindicich N, White N. *Australian drug trends 2007: Findings from the illicit drug reporting system (IDRS).* Sydney: National Drug and Alcohol Research Centre, University of New South Wales; 2008.

19. Imrie J, Frankland A (eds.). *HIV/AIDS, hepatitis and sexually transmissible infections in Australia: Annual report of trends in behaviour 2008.* Sydney: National Centre in HIV Social Research, University of New South Wales; 2008:29, 31.

20. Richters J, Song A, Prestage GP, Calyton S, Turner R. *Health of lesbian, bisexual and queer women in Sydney: The 2004 Sydney Women and Sexual Health survey.* Sydney: National Centre in HIV Social Research; 2005.

21. Richters J, Butler T, Yap L, Kirkwood K, Grant L, Smith A, Schneider K, Donovan B. *Sexual health and behaviour of New South Wales prisoners.* Sydney: School of Public Health and Community Medicine, University of New South Wales; 2008:26.

22. Hall W, Nelson J. Correlates of the perceived health risks of marijuana use among Australian adults. *Drug Alcohol Rev* 1996; 15:137–43.

23. Smith AM, Pitts MK, Shelley JM, Richters J, Ferris J. The Australian longitudinal study of health and relationships. *BMC Public Health* 2007; 7:139.

24. Laumann EO, Paik A, Rosen RC. Sexual dysfunction in the United States: Prevalence and predictors. *JAMA* 1999; 281:537–44.

25. Mercer CH, Fenton KA, Johnson AM, Wellings K, Macdowall W, McManus S, Nanchahal K, Erens B. Sexual function problems and help seeking behaviour in Britain: National probability sample survey. *BMJ* 2003; 327:426–7.

26. Richters J, Grulich AE, De Visser RO, Smith AM, Rissel CE. Sex in Australia: Sexual difficulties in a representative sample of adults. *Aust N Z J Public Health* 2003; 27:164–70.

27. De Visser RO, Smith AM, Rissel CE, Richters J, Grulich AE. Sex in Australia: Safer sex and condom use among a representative sample of adults. *Aust N Z J Public Health* 2003; 27:223–9.

28. De Visser RO, Smith AM, Rissel CE, Richters J, Grulich AE. Sex in Australia: Heterosexual experience and recent heterosexual encounters among a representative sample of adults. *Aust N Z J Public Health* 2003; 27:146–54.

29. Grulich AE, De Visser RO, Smith AM, Rissel CE, Richters J. Sex in Australia: Sexually transmissible infection and blood-borne virus history in a representative sample of adults. *Aust N Z J Public Health* 2003; 27:234–41.

30. Grulich AE, De Visser RO, Smith AM, Rissel CE, Richters J. Sex in Australia: Homosexual experience and recent homosexual encounters. *Aust N Z J Public Health* 2003; 27:155–63.

31. StataCorp LP. *Stata statistical software: Release 10. [program].* College Station, TX: StataCorp LP; 2007.

32. Buffum J. Pharmacosexology: The effects of drugs on sexual function. *J Psychoactive Drugs* 1982; 14:5–44.

33. Halikas J, Weller R, Morse C. Effects of regular marijuana use on sexual performance. *J Psychoactive Drugs* 1982; 14:59–70.

| "The sexual effects of alcohol, cocaine, narcotics, and meth—you name it— are well documented and predictable. But not marijuana."

Marijuana's Effects on Sex Vary with Individuals

Michael Castleman

Michael Castleman is a journalist and the author of Great Sex: A Man's Guide to the Secret Principles of Total-Body Sex. *In the following viewpoint, he reports on an informal survey of readers at PsychologyToday.com focusing on the sexual effects of marijuana. He says that the majority of readers felt marijuana enhanced sex, while a minority said that it hurt their sex lives. Castleman was most interested in a group of respondents who said that marijuana's effect on sex depended on the type of marijuana and/or the circumstances surrounding their sexual encounters. He suggests that more research should be done on the possibility that marijuana's sexual effects are variable.*

As you read, consider the following questions:

1. What drugs have predictable sexual effects, according to Castleman?

2. Why does Castleman say that his survey cannot provide a definitive answer to the question of marijuana's effect on sexuality?

3. What value does Castleman say anecdotes may have for research?

A year ago [in 2010], I posted about marijuana's contradictory effects on lovemaking, an impact notably different from other recreational drugs. The sexual effects of alcohol, cocaine, narcotics, and meth—you name it—are well documented and predictable. But not marijuana. Its sexual effects are all over the map, from "I can't stand having sex stoned," to "I never have sex without it."

Effects Vary

In the literature, those who call weed sex-inhibiting typically say that when stoned, they withdraw into themselves and lose the connection to their partner. Those who call pot sex-enhancing usually say that it boosts desire, increases arousal, enhances sensuality, and helps them feel closer to their partner.

Research into the sexual impact of marijuana dates from the 1970s. One of the first reports showed that it reduces testosterone enough to impair libido in many women and some men. But in short order, that study was thoroughly debunked.

Subsequent studies showed that weed has wildly contradictory effects on sex. A 1984 report found that it enhanced lovemaking in two-thirds of respondents, but ruined it in the other third. Studies from 2003 and 2008 show that about half called the drug sex-enhancing, while half said it was not.

A year ago, I put this question to readers: How does marijuana affect *your* sex life?

I make no claim that the comments readers posted represent a definitive answer to the question. Obviously, replies were self-selected, not random, and not demographically representative. Nonetheless, they're intriguing, largely because beyond saying that marijuana either improves or detracts from sex, quite a few respondents said something that has so far not turned up in the literature, "It depends."

67% of respondents said marijuana enhances sex.

- "I'm not a frequent smoker, but when I have smoked and then had sex, it's been the most amazing sex of my life."

- "Marijuana engulfs me in sex foam. I'm just pure sex on that stuff. It's great. I could never feel that way sober or drunk."

- "Definitely enhances sex. A few tokes make me feel horny the vast majority of the time, and it makes the whole experience much more enjoyable."

- "After smoking, I can feel my nipples perk up, clitoris tingle, and vagina become wet to the point that I can feel it through my pants and my man knows he is in for a *LONG* night."

- "Cannabis is soooo good for sex that sometimes it can become awkward because during casual hookups, the woman might get the wrong idea. . . ."

12% said marijuana destroys sex.

- "My boyfriend and I have smoked (fairly heavily) for the past year and I would say that it 100% has a terrible effect on our sex life. It's been a huge libido killer for our relationship."

- "As I've continued to use marijuana (been almost 5 years smoking now) it's inhibited sex for me more and more."

Marijuana and Enhanced Orgasms

The most characteristic effect related to sex for [C.T.] Tart's (1971) participants concerned enhanced orgasm. Users reported that they appreciated new qualities of orgasm that they did not usually experience when sober. This effect may parallel a general increase in the excitement, joy, and sensitivity of touch, which was also characteristic of intoxication in this sample. Over half of the participants reported that they were better lovers after using the drug, with many suggesting that they were more responsive and giving. Most of these effects did not begin until at least a moderate degree of intoxication.

Mitch Earleywine,
Understanding Marijuana:
A New Look at the Scientific Evidence.
New York: Oxford University Press, 2002.

It Depends

But 20% said marijuana's sexual effect depends on the dose, strain, and the smoker's mood.

- "The effects of marijuana strongly relate to how a person is feeling prior to smoking. If I'm in a bad mood and smoke, sex is completely out of the question because, as you said, I withdraw into myself and just can't connect with anyone else. On the other hand, if my beau and I have had a great night out and top it off with a bowl, it's definitely got its merits."

- "Contrary to popular belief, not all buds are alike. Some weed makes you want to be very sexual and I've had some of the best orgasms of my life after using marijuana. Some of it makes you feel more introverted and thoughtful."

- "I find that indica shortly before sex is just unbeatable for mind-blowing lovemaking. Sativa should be avoided as its cerebral nature will make your mind wander."

As I mentioned, these comments can't be seen as anything other than anecdotal reports. But anecdotes often stimulate more rigorous research. If any research psychologists or psychopharmacologists read this and are [planning] to study marijuana's impact on sex, I suggest that you include the option "it depends." Clearly, many PsychologyToday.com readers think it does.

Periodical and Internet Sources Bibliography

The following articles have been selected to supplement the diverse views presented in this chapter.

Jillian Aramowicz	"Marijuana Not as Dangerous as Most Legal Drugs," *Kansas State Collegian*, December 2, 2010.
Ewen Callaway	"Regular Marijuana Usage Robs Men of Sexual Highs," *New Scientist*, August 2009.
Michael Castleman	"How Does Marijuana Affect YOUR Sex Life?," *All About Sex—Psychology Today*, March 30, 2010. www.psychologytoday.com.
CNN	"Report: Depressed Teens, Marijuana a Dangerous Mix," May 9, 2008. http://article.cnn.com.
Kevin Fagan	"How Healthy—or Dangerous—Is Marijuana Use?," *San Francisco Chronicle*, July 18, 2010.
Charles V. Giannasio	"Marijuana Is Addictive, Destructive and Dangerous," CNBC, April 20, 2010. www.cnbc.com.
Aina Hunter	"Marijuana a 'Gateway' Drug? Scientists Call Theory Half-Baked," CBS News, September 2, 2010. www.cbsnews.com.
Sarah Kershaw and Rebecca Cathcart	"Marijuana Is Gateway Drug for Two Debates," *New York Times*, July 17, 2009.
ScienceDaily	"Marijuana Smokers Face Rapid Lung Destruction—as Much as 20 Years Ahead of Tobacco Smokers," January 27, 2008. www.sciencedaily.com.
Maia Szalavitz	"Marijuana as a Gateway Drug: The Myth That Will Not Die," *Time*, October 29, 2010.

OPPOSING VIEWPOINTS® SERIES

CHAPTER 2

Are There Medical Benefits to Using Marijuana?

Chapter Preface

Migraines—intense, throbbing headaches—may be accompanied by loss of vision or flashing lights and can result in nausea or vomiting. The cause of migraines is uncertain, though most researchers think they are due to abnormal changes in levels of substances that are naturally produced in the brain.

Marijuana was often used to treat migraine headaches in the 1800s, according to *Marijuana Medical Handbook: Practical Guide to the Therapeutic Uses of Marijuana* by Dale Gieringer, Ed Rosenthal, and Gregory T. Carter. Gieringer and his colleagues note that today "many patients find that marijuana is more effective than conventional prescription drugs" in treating migraines. They add, "There is some evidence that THC [the active ingredient in marijuana] . . . inhibits the release of serotonin from blood platelet cells, a likely causal factor in migraines." The authors also note that in some cases marijuana appears to trigger migraines.

Alison Mack and Janet Joy, in *Marijuana as Medicine? The Science Beyond the Controversy*, express skepticism about the use of marijuana to cure migraines. They say that as of 2005, they had found only a single scientific study about marijuana and migraines. The study consisted "of a description of three cases in which people suffered migraines after quitting their daily marijuana habits." Mack and Joy argue, "This is hardly convincing evidence that marijuana relieves migraine pain, since it is equally likely that the headaches were caused by withdrawal from the drug."

Mack and Joy contend that more research is needed on the links between migraines and marijuana. However, restrictive government policies on marijuana research may prevent such studies, at least in the near future.

In this chapter, viewpoints address potential benefits and drawbacks of proposed medical uses of marijuana for the treatment of other conditions such as pain, childhood autism, and nausea during pregnancy.

> *"Numerous studies have now established that cannabinoids help lessen pain and affect a wide range of symptoms and bodily functions."*

Marijuana Can Help in the Treatment of Pain

Bill McCarberg

Bill McCarberg is founder of the Chronic Pain Management Program for Kaiser Permanente. In the following viewpoint, he says that cannabinoids found in marijuana have been shown to be effective in reducing pain. He notes that much more clinical study is required and that it is difficult to balance the intoxicating and pain relieving effects of marijuana. Nonetheless, he concludes that cannabinoid pain relievers are very promising and hopes that they will soon become an important medical therapy for pain.

As you read, consider the following questions:

1. What are the three informal categories of cannabinoid, according to McCarberg?

2. What problems does McCarberg say arise when taking cannabinoids orally?

3. According to McCarberg, what problems are there with the quality of herbal cannabis sold through dispensaries?

Millions of people in the United States suffer from chronic pain, and much of that suffering cannot be relieved adequately by existing treatments. Patients are in desperate need of new pain management approaches. Cannabinoid medicines appear very promising, although the subject often is obscured by controversy, prejudice, and confusion in part because cannabinoids have some relation to the cannabis plant—also known by the slang term marijuana.

Do Cannabinoids Work?

What scientific reasons do doctors have to think that cannabinoids actually work? Do they provide genuine symptom improvement, or do patients become intoxicated and merely think that their symptoms are reduced?

Basic research conducted over the past 20 years provides us with many answers. In the early 1990s, researchers identified the cannabinoid receptor system. This system is found in some of the most primitive animal forms on earth—it is also the most widespread receptor system in the human body.

The cannabinoid receptor system has two types of receptors:

- CB1 receptors are found primarily in the brain, spinal cord, and periphery.

- CB2 receptors are on the immune tissues.

Specific molecules (called endocannabinoids) are produced by the body that interact with these CB1 and CB2 receptors, much like endorphins interact with the body's opioid receptor system. These findings initiated a new era of scientific interest and research in cannabinoids.

Numerous studies have now established that cannabinoids help lessen pain and affect a wide range of symptoms and bodily functions. Such research has also demonstrated that cannabinoids may work together with opioids to enhance their effectiveness and reduce tolerance.

This body of research has allowed cannabinoids to be informally classified into three types:

- endocannabinoids (produced by the body)

- phytocannabinoids (produced by the cannabis plant)

- synthetic cannabinoids (produced in the laboratory)

Each type is being studied aggressively, but because endocannabinoids are quickly metabolized and probably cannot be patented, they have not yet been researched in humans.

What progress is being made toward developing cannabinoids as prescription pain relievers? Some cannabinoids are unstable and many are insoluble in water, which makes them difficult to research and turn into modern medicines. Patients react very differently to cannabinoids. Data from recent clinical trials are encouraging, but somewhat mixed. Looking closely at the results suggests that composition and delivery route (i.e., how a medicine is administered) are extremely important to the viability of cannabinoid medicines.

The Delivery Route

When taken orally, cannabinoids are not very well absorbed and often have unpredictable effects. Patients often become sedated or have intoxication-like symptoms when tetrahydrocannabinol (THC—the primary psychoactive cannabinoid in cannabis) is metabolized by the liver. A small number of studies with Marinol (synthetic THC in sesame oil in a gelatin capsule) and Cesamet (synthetic THC analogue) have shown some effectiveness in pain relief, but optimal doses that relieve pain often cannot be achieved because of unpleasant psychologic side effects.

Marijuana Use with Chronic Pain

Marijuana is another analgesic that has been around for many centuries. Cannabis is currently and rather recently illegal in many countries including the United States. Still, probably about 10–20 percent of . . . patients admit to trying marijuana as a pain reliever for their chronic pain. Most of them report significant pain relief. Some comment that it is their most effective pain reliever.

Tim Sams, ABC's of Pain Relief and Treatment: Advances, Breakthroughs, and Choices. *Lincoln, NE: iUniverse, 2006.*

Inhaling cannabinoids, especially THC, also may cause problems for many patients. Blood levels rise suddenly and then drop off sharply. This rapid on-off effect may produce significant intoxication, particularly in patients who are new to cannabinoids. This may pose the risk of abuse potential. Smoking cannabis produces this effect, which is the very reason that recreational users prefer the inhaled route. Patients, however, generally wish to avoid psychologic effects, and it is unclear how difficult it might be to find a dosing pattern that enables them to have pain control without side effects.

A new product, called Sativex, was approved by Health Canada in June 2005 for marketing as an adjunctive medicine for central neuropathic pain in multiple sclerosis. Adjunctive therapy means taking two or more medications to help control pain.

Sativex has a different delivery system—an oromucosal/sublingual spray absorbed by the lining of the mouth—that, according to the manufacturer, generally allows patients to gradually work up to a stable dose at which they obtain therapeutic pain relief without unwanted psychologic effects.

In the United States, Sativex is being studied in large randomized trials in cancer pain that has not been adequately relieved by opioids. Three early and six pivotal controlled studies in the United Kingdom demonstrated positive results treating chronic pain of various origins including neurologic pain, various symptoms of multiple sclerosis, rheumatoid arthritis, and cancer pain. Initial results show improvement in pain for more than one year despite lack of effectiveness of the opioids. Common adverse effects of Savitex have included complaints of bad taste, stinging, dry mouth, dizziness, nausea or fatigue.

Additional research also may uncover other ways of avoiding the problems associated with oral or inhaled delivery. Ajulemic acid, a synthetic cannabinoid, binds to both the CB1 and CB2 receptors, and has shown benefit in a small neuropathic pain trial. It may have reduced psychologic effects and is being studied for the treatment of interstitial cystitis.

Research Is Promising

The use of herbal cannabis—usually smoked—has received considerable media attention since California and Arizona passed "medical marijuana" initiatives in 1996. Despite numerous anecdotal reports of effectiveness, very few controlled studies have been published in the pain area. Little is known about the number of patients who actually experience some degree of benefit or side effects.

Furthermore, herbal cannabis is neither standardized nor monitored for quality. The cannabinoid content can vary a great deal, and cannabis sold at dispensaries may be contaminated with pesticides or mold. Dosing is uncertain, depending on the preparation or method of use. So-called "vaporizers" do not eliminate all the contaminants. Without clinical trial data and an assurance of product quality, physicians lack the information necessary to assist patients in making informed therapeutic decisions. Both the FDA [US Food and Drug Administration] and Institute of Medicine have stated that there is no future for herbal cannabis as a prescription medicine.

Nevertheless, there may be some truth to the idea that there is pain relief potential in phytocannabinoids (plant-based cannabinoids) and that such potential may be affected by the interaction of THC with other botanical components, particularly with other cannabinoids. Modern strains of cannabis have been bred to maximize the THC at the expense of all other cannabinoids, most of which do not have psychologic effects. Some of those cannabinoids, such as cannabidiol (CBD), have been demonstrated to have important therapeutic value, particularly on pain and inflammation.

The possibilities for cannabinoid medicines are very promising, and much exciting research is proceeding at a rapid pace. As new FDA-approved cannabinoid products become available, physicians and patients will have a solid scientific foundation from which to assess their appropriateness. Hopefully, robust scientific data will soon allow cannabinoids to take their place—along with opiates and other pain relievers—in the modern medical supply for treating chronic pain.

> *"If you had a toothache, you probably wouldn't want to treat it with marijuana, because you could actually make it worse."*

Marijuana Use Can Increase Pain

Medical News Today

Medical News Today *is an Internet health news publication. In the following viewpoint,* Medical News Today *reports on a study that found that active ingredients such as those in marijuana tend to prolong pain.* Medical News Today *noted that this was surprising since marijuana is often said to relieve pain. Researchers said that marijuana may be useful in some situations but conclude that it should be used with great care for pain relief in light of the study.*

As you read, consider the following questions:

1. What are endocannabinoids, and how do they affect pain, according to the viewpoint?

2. What is capsaicin, and how does this viewpoint say it was used to study pain effects?

3. Under what circumstances might marijuana be useful in treating pain, according to Professor Neugebauer?

Imagine that you're working on your back porch, hammering in a nail. Suddenly you slip and hit your thumb instead—hard. The pain is incredibly intense, but it only lasts a moment. After a few seconds (and a few unprintable words) you're ready to start hammering again.

Understanding Pain

How can such severe pain vanish so quickly? And why is it that other kinds of equally terrible pain refuse to go away, and instead torment their victims for years?

University of Texas Medical Branch [UTMB] at Galveston researchers think they've found at least part of the answer—and believe it or not, it's in a group of compounds that includes the active ingredients in marijuana, the cannabinoids. Interestingly enough, given recent interest in the medical use of marijuana for pain relief, experiments with rodents and humans described in a paper published in the current issue of *Science* suggest these "endocannabinoids," which are made within the human body, can actually amplify and prolong pain rather than damping it down.

"In the spinal cord there's a balance of systems that control what information, including information about pain, is transmitted to the brain," said UTMB professor Volker Neugebauer, one of the authors of the *Science* article, along with UTMB senior research scientist Guangchen Ji and collaborators from Switzerland, Hungary, Japan, Germany, France and Venezuela. "Excitatory systems act like a car's accelerator, and inhibitory ones act like the brakes. What we found is that in the spinal cord endocannabinoids can disable the brakes."

To get to this conclusion, the researchers began by studying what happened when they applied a biochemical mimic of an endocannabinoid to inhibitory neurons (the brakes, in

Neugebauer's analogy) on slices of mouse spinal cord. Electrical signals that would ordinarily have elicited an inhibitory response were ignored. They then repeated the procedure using slices of spinal cord from mice genetically engineered to lack receptors where the endocannabinoid molecules could dock, and found that in that case, the "brakes" worked. Finally, using electron microscopy, they confirmed that the receptors were in fact on inhibitory, not excitatory neurons. Endocannabinoids docking with them would suppress the inhibitor neurons, and leave pain signals with a straight shot to the brain.

"The next step was to make the leap from spinal slices to test whether this really had anything to do with pain," Neugebauer said. Using anesthetized rats, he recorded the spinal cord electrical activity produced by an injection in the hindpaw of capsaicin—a chemical found in hot peppers that produces a level of pain he compared to a severe toothache. Although the rats were unconscious, pain impulses could be detected racing up their spinal cords. What's more, formerly benign stimuli now generated a significant pain response—a response that stopped when the rats were treated with an endocannabinoid receptor blocker.

"Why was this non-painful information now gaining access to the spinal 'pain' neurons?" Neugebauer said. "The capsaicin produced an overstimulation that led to the peripheral nerves releasing endocannabinoids, which activated receptors that shut down the inhibitor neurons, leaving the gates wide open."

Human Tests

Finally, the researchers recruited human volunteers to determine whether a compound that blocked endocannabinoid receptors would have an effect on the increased sensitivity to pain (hyperalgesia) and tendency for normally non-painful stimuli to induce pain (allodynia) often reported in areas of the body near where acute pain had been inflicted. In this case, the researchers induced pain by passing electricity through the volunteers' left forearms, with the intensity of the current set by each volunteer to a 6 on a scale of 1 to 10. At a second session a month later, the volunteers who had received the receptor blocker showed no reduction in perceived acute pain, but had significantly less hyperalgesia and allodynia—a result that matched up well with the endocannabinoid hypothesis.

"To sum up, we've discovered a novel mechanism that can transform transient normal pain into persistent chronic pain," Neugebauer said. "Persistent pain is notoriously difficult to treat, and this study offers insight into new mechanisms and possibly a new target in the spinal cord."

It also raises questions about the efficacy of marijuana in relieving acute pain, given that endocannabinoids and the cannabinoids found in marijuana are so biochemically similar. "If you had a toothache, you probably wouldn't want to treat it with marijuana, because you could actually make it worse," Neugebauer said. "Now, for more pathological conditions like neuropathic pain, where the problem is a dysfunction within the nerves themselves and a subsequent disturbance throughout the nervous system that's not confined to the pain system, marijuana may be beneficial. There are studies that seem to show that. But our model shows cannabinoids over-activating the pain system, and it just doesn't seem like a good idea to further increase this effect."

> "I am grateful that the cannabis has given J. the chance to get out and experience life. If it sometimes punches him back, it also offers him flowers."

Marijuana Helps with Autism

Marie Myung-Ok Lee

Marie Myung-Ok Lee is an award-winning novelist and essayist who teaches at Brown University. In the following viewpoint, Lee discusses her decision to treat her nine-year-old autistic son with cannabis. She reports that the cannabis has had a dramatic effect on her son's behavior, controlling his constant pain, controlling his compulsive eating, and eliminating his violent outbursts. She notes that some symptoms, such as vocalizations, remain but concludes that cannabis has allowed her son to function in most respects as a happy, healthy, pain-free child.

As you read, consider the following questions:

1. What is pica, according to Lee?

2. What does Lee say had been the most traumatic and unpredictable moment of the day for the last few years, and why?

3. According to Lee, how did J. respond to being offered *doenjang* soup pre-cannabis, and how did his reaction differ after his treatment was established?

L ast spring, I wrote about applying for a medical marijuana license for my autistic, allergic 9-year-old son, J., in hopes of soothing his gut pain and anxiety, the roots of the behavioral demons that caused him to lash out at others and himself. After reading studies of how cannabis can ease pain and worry, and in consultation with his doctor, we decided to give it a try. A month into daily cannabis tea and mj-oil cookies (my husband discovered his inner baker), I reported, we both felt that J. *seemed* happier. But it was hard to tell. He'd have a good morning, then at dinner he'd throw his food. Still, we did notice that when he came home from school with stomach pain (he wasn't getting any supplemental cannabis there), he'd run to the kitchen and demand his tea and cookie. As if he knew this was the stuff that dulled the hellish gut pangs.

Improvement After Four Months

How is J. doing now, four months into our cannabis experiment? Well, one day recently, he came home from school, and I noticed something really different: He had a whole shirt on.

Pre-pot, J. ate things that weren't food. There's a name for this: pica. (Pregnant women are known to pica on chalk and laundry starch.) J. chewed the collar of his T-shirts while stealthily deconstructing them from the bottom up, teasing apart and then swallowing the threads. By the time I picked him up from the bus stop after school, the front half of his shirt was gone. His pica become so uncontrollable we couldn't let him sleep with a pajama top (it would be gone by morning) or a pillow (ditto the case and the stuffing). An antique family quilt was reduced to fabric strips, and he even managed to eat holes in a fleece blanket—so much for his organic diet. I started dressing him only in organic cotton shirts, but we couldn't support the cost of a new one every day. The worst part was watching him scream in pain on the toilet, when what went in had to come out. I had nightmares about long threads knotting in digestive organs. (TMI [too much information]? Welcome to our life!)

Reduced Aggression

Almost immediately after we started the cannabis, the pica stopped. Just stopped. J. now sleeps with his organic wool-and-cotton, hypoallergenic, temptingly chewable comforter. He pulls it up to his chin at night and declares, "I'm cozy!"

Next, we started seeing changes in J.'s school reports. His curriculum is based on a therapy called Applied Behavior Analysis, which involves, as the name implies, meticulous analysis of data. At one parent meeting in August [2009] (J. is on an extended school year), his teacher excitedly presented his June–July "aggression" chart. An aggression is defined as any attempt or instance of hitting, kicking, biting, or pinching another person. For the past year, he'd consistently had 30 to 50 aggressions in a school day, with a one-time high of 300. The charts for June through July, by contrast, showed he was actually having days—sometimes one after another—with *zero* aggressions.

More evidence: the bus. For the last few years, the arrival of J.'s school bus had been the most traumatic and unpredictable moment of our day. J. has run onto the bus and hit the driver in the face. He has scuffled with the aides and tried to bite them. His behavior brought out the worst in people: One bus monitor (we joked that her personality better suited her for a job at the local prison) seemed to dislike all the kids but treated him with particular contempt, even calling him names, once in front of us.

But the summer brought a new set of aides and driver. It hit me that these folks knew only "Cannabis J."—a sparkly

J's First Marijuana Treatment

We made the cookies with the marijuana olive oil, starting J. off with half a small cookie, eaten after dinner. J. normally goes to bed around 7:30 p.m.; by 6:30 he declared he was tired and conked out. We checked on him hourly. As we anxiously peeked in, half-expecting some red-eyed ogre from *Reefer Madness* to come leaping out at us, we saw instead that he was sleeping peacefully. Usually, his sleep is shallow and restless. J. also woke up happy.

Marie Myung-Ok Lee,
"Why I Give My 9-Year-Old Pot,"
Slate, *May 11, 2009.*

eyed boy who says hi to them each morning, goes quietly to his seat, even tries to help put his snap-on harness on.

One day, J.'s regular aide was sick, and a lady with a wacky smile lovingly escorted J. off the bus. There was something familiar about her; once I superimposed a hateful frown on her face, I burst out to my husband, as the bus snorted away, "It was *her*, wasn't it?" We laughed as J. looked on. "Funny!" he said.

Symptoms Remain

There's a twist to the happy marijuana story, though. While the cannabis has eased J.'s most overwhelming problem, his autism has become more distinct. As the school data show, his aggressive behavior is far less frequent, but his outbursts—vocalizations that include screams, barking, yips of happiness—remain. When J. was in his dark phase, we spent our time out of sight, out of mind, inside our house with a screeching, violent, food-and-dish-flinging J. The sounds were contained by double-paned windows (when they weren't broken). Now, within our family, we've reached a lovely homeostasis: household goods unbroken, our arms and J.'s face unscratched. But as we venture outside to play in the yard, take after-dinner walks, or ride with J. on our tandem bike, we can see that the people in the neighborhood know our family is different, and that this is not always to their liking.

Our closest neighbors (on one side, we could probably pass them a pie from our kitchen) have always been understanding. But on the next street, a man stops playing ball with his son when he sees us, and pushes his boy into the house as we approach, turning his back on J.'s cheery "hel-llooo!" He is the man we suspect yells at us—from behind other houses, so we can't see him—when J. sometimes vocalizes a bit loudly outside. Then there's the mom with the son about J.'s age (who, incidentally, sounds *exactly* like J. when he screams). She won't make eye contact when we pass, and pointedly ignored a party invitation from us. I've also heard, from behind a fence of a family who stares at us but never says hi, "Oh, that's J."

And so sometimes we feel a bit the victims of a 21st-century shunning. In the larger context, however, these are small annoyances from small people. The chair of my department invites J. to *her* yard so he can play in her outdoor pool and lets him vocalize to her neighbors, who do not complain. A mini-gang of too-cool teen boys walks by our short fence after school and always greets J. sincerely, as he calls out adoringly, "Hi, hi, HIIIIIIIIII!" I am grateful that the cannabis has given J. the chance to get out and experience life. If it sometimes punches him back, it also offers him flowers.

I don't consider marijuana a miracle cure for autism. But as an amateur herbalist, I do consider it a wonderful, safe botanical that allows J. to participate more fully in life without the dangers and sometimes permanent side effects of pharmaceutical drugs; now that we have a good dose and a good strain. ("White Russian"—a favorite of cancer patients, who also need relief from extreme pain). Free from pain, J. can go to school and learn. And his violent behavior won't put him in the local children's psychiatric hospital—a scenario all too common among his peers.

A friend whose child was once diagnosed with autism, but no longer (he attends school at his grade level and had three developmental assessments showing he no longer merits the diagnosis), wanted to embark on a kind of karmic mission to help other children. After extensive research, she landed on cannabis the way I had. "It has dramatic implications for the autism community," she says, and it's true. We have pictures of J. from a year ago when he would actually claw at his own face. None of the experts had a clue what to do. That little child with the horrifically bleeding and scabbed face looks to us now like a visitor from another world. The J. we know now doesn't look stoned. He just looks like a happy little boy.

More Surprises

And cannabis still can surprise us. We worried that "the munchies" would severely aggravate J.'s problems with overeating in response to his stomach pangs. Instead, the marijuana seems to have modulated these symptoms. Perhaps the pain signals from his stomach were coming through as hunger. J. still can get overexcited if he likes a food too much, so sometimes when he's eating my husband and I leave the room to minimize distractions. The other day, we dared to experiment with *doenjang*, a fermented tofu soup that he used to love as a baby. The last time we tried it, a year ago, he'd frisbeed the bowl against a tile wall. (Oh, smelly *doenjang* soup and the million ways it can make a mess.)

We left J. in the kitchen with his steamy bowl and went to the adjoining room. We waited. We heard the spoon ding against the bowl. Satisfied slurpy noises. Then a strange noise that we couldn't identify. A *chkka chkka chkkka bsssshhht doinnng!* We returned to the kitchen, half expecting to see the walls painted with *doenjang.* Everything was clean. The bowl and spoon, however, were gone.

J. had taken his dishes to the sink, rinsed them, and put them in the dishwasher—something we'd never shown him how to do, though he must have watched us do it a million times. In four months, he'd gone from a boy we couldn't feed to a boy who could feed himself and clean up after. The sight of the bowl, not quite rinsed, but almost, was one of the sweetest sights of my parental life. I expect more to come.

> "Parents who resort to using marijuana as an aid with their autistic child risk raising a child addicted to marijuana and ill prepared for adulthood."

Marijuana Is Dangerous for Autism Sufferers

Ugo Uche

Ugo Uche is a licensed professional counselor who specializes in adolescents and young adults. In the following viewpoint, he argues that using marijuana to treat autism is ineffective and dangerous. He says that autistic children have difficulty relating to others and that marijuana has been shown to reduce the ability to perceive emotions in others. Thus, he says, marijuana may exacerbate autism's effects. He argues that parents must treat autism with behavioral techniques rigorously applied. This is difficult, he says, but using marijuana instead may result in a child who is addicted to marijuana and unprepared for adult life.

As you read, consider the following questions:

1. Why is Uche reluctant to say what steps the mother in the news report he discusses should have taken to treat her son's self-starvation?

Ugo Uche, "Does Marijuana Really Help Autistic Children and Adolescents Cope with Their Symptoms?," *Psychology Today*, November 30, 2009. Copyright © 2009 by Sussex Publishers LLC. All rights reserved. Reproduced by permission.

2. According to Uche, why would marijuana interfere with the ability to cure autistic children of repetitive patterns of behavior?

3. Why does Uche believe that behavioral techniques in some families fail to correct autism?

A number of years ago as a therapist in a state-sponsored residential treatment program, we found ourselves in a heated dispute. On the discussion table were two camps, the first which I belonged to had to do with getting rid of the organization's policy to physically restrain a youth if he acted out and presented as a threat to himself or his peers, and the second camp was about maintaining the organization's policy.

Taking the Easy Route

The problem with this organization's policy was that students became subject to being restrained even if they found themselves in a pushing contest with another peer, and as one of my coworkers put it plainly, "by not doing away with the physical restraint rule, we were simply trying to make our jobs easier, without making a true impact in the lives to the students we were there to help." I was recently reminded of this statement, when I encountered the news story of a mother who reportedly gave her autistic son marijuana to address his refusal to eat, and I also suspect—rage episodes. It is no secret what my stance on marijuana is, and that of some readers who vehemently disagree with me. Needless to write, this mother is absolutely wrong in her actions, and she is taking the easy route in addressing her son's mental health issues.

True, I understand that marijuana is notorious for increasing appetite in consumers of the drug, which would make sense for the case of her ten-year-old son, who wasn't eating. However, there are a number of alternatives she as a mother could have taken to address her son's refusal to eat. I would go into what these steps are, as I expect an irritate[d] reader will demand to know. However I am reluctant, as I am not aware of the specifics of the boy's self-starvation. Different circumstances call for different measures. What I would like to get into are the primary symptoms of autism and why marijuana doesn't help.

There are three significant symptoms an autistic child suffers from, and these are problems in socially relating to others, qualitative impairments in communicating and restrictive repetitive, stereotyped patterns of behavior. Marijuana does not improve any of these symptoms. According to the National Institute on Drug Abuse, there are eleven research studies which suggest that heavy marijuana use (defined by smoking marijuana for twenty-seven consecutive days or more) leads to a decline in a person's ability to learn, retain information and function successfully in society. Being able to socially relate to others in diverse settings is learned behavior, so for a child who already struggles with this skill, marijuana decreases the likelihood that any progress will be made on the issue.

Behavioral Techniques Are Needed

Furthermore, in a 1978 research study conducted by Paul Clopton and his colleagues on "marijuana and the perception of effect." The results of this study strongly suggested that consumption of marijuana significantly reduced an individual's ability to perceive emotions in others. Needless to say, the ability for one person to perceive emotions in another involves empathy on the perceiver's part and for empathy to be present; communication also has to be present. Yet another reason why giving marijuana to an autistic child is a poor medical decision, as the likelihood of a child's being able to improve upon poor communication skills is significantly reduced. The third symptom of autism in children which has to do with restrictive, repetitive and stereotyped patterns of behaviors, all have to do with the child or adolescent developing an awareness on how certain socially unacceptable behaviors can put others off, and can cause a child to experience excessive episodes of rejection. Again being able to read social cues, all comes down to being empathetic.

In all fairness, this isn't the first mother who claims that marijuana has helped her a great deal in being able to manage her son's autism. In my research I found several stories of mothers who claimed that marijuana did miracles for their children suffering with autism, however, there were also several mothers who reported that behavioral measures had mixed results—for good reason. By one mother's account, she admitted that behavioral measures for her had mixed results, due to inconsistencies in practice. According to her, she and her husband found the behavioral techniques they had learned from their son's therapist too cumbersome and laborious.

Unfortunately, that's the nature of the beast; behavioral techniques, even for autistic children, do work. However, in order for them to work, they have to be practiced a hundred percent of the time, and this will call for a radical change in the lifestyles of the parents. The purpose of raising a child is to prepare them for the stress and added responsibilities of adulthood; parents who resort to using marijuana as an aid with their autistic child risk raising a child addicted to marijuana and ill prepared for adulthood.

> "Did I eventually break down and try marijuana? You bet. Did it work? Yes. Do I feel guilty about it? Not a single bit."

Marijuana Can Help with Nausea During Pregnancy

Amie Newman

Amie Newman is a communications officer at the Bill and Melinda Gates Foundation. In the following viewpoint, she says that many women have obtained relief from severe, sometimes life-threatening nausea in pregnancy by using marijuana. She argues that the demonization of marijuana by antidrug advocates is unjust and unfair to women. She says that medical expert opinion indicates that marijuana used medicinally is not a serious danger to unborn children. She concludes that women's choices should be respected and that the health of the mother and child should be put above ideological antidrug policy.

As you read, consider the following questions:

1. What is hyperemesis gravidarum and why can it be dangerous, according to the viewpoint?

2. According to Newman, what happened to Anita Baker after she tested positive for marijuana when she delivered twins in 2004?

3. Why did Melanie Dreher perform her marijuana and pregnancy studies in Jamaica?

Stumble upon any number of online communities for pregnant women and you can't help but find women, mostly in their first trimester, spilling their guts (figuratively) about the fact that they're spilling their guts regularly and feel as if they want to die daily from the nausea, inability to keep down food or drinks and the constant vomiting.

Vomiting and Malnutrition

According to the Mayo Clinic's Mary Murry, anywhere between 50 to 90 percent of pregnant women experience some nausea—to varying degrees. For most women, the nausea peaks, says Murry, around nine weeks and ends by about the 18th or 19th week of pregnancy. For five percent of unlucky women, however, it persists until the bitter end. It's hardly surprising. If you've been pregnant or know someone who has, it's likely that the saccharine sweet euphemism "morning sickness" doesn't do justice to what you or your friends have felt. For some pregnant women, the nausea passes quickly and easily. For others it becomes a daily—or even hourly—battle between one's body and one's intellectual understanding that if one doesn't consume a crumb of food at some point one will slowly starve or starve one's poor, growing embryo or fetus. This condition is called hyperemesis gravidarum and the constant vomiting and nausea lead to extreme weight loss and even malnutrition for the woman. It's dangerous.

If there's one theorem I can prove, however, it's this: for every pregnant woman in the world who's experienced any symptom or discomfort under the sun, there [are] a million different suggestions for treatment. But what happens when one of those suggestions is the use of an illegal substance?

When it comes to nausea and vomiting, women experiment to be sure: from prescription medication to concoctions of ginger tea and herbs to acupressure wristbands and more. When you're experiencing what one pregnant woman posting on the Mayo Clinic's pregnancy blog experienced, you're willing to try almost anything.

> I'm 13 weeks into this and haven't had a day of peace in over 7 weeks (it was 7 weeks this past Thursday, yes, I'm keeping count). *I've been nauseated and throwing up to the point of going in for weekly IVs for 5 weeks now.* I couldn't wait to get pregnant and now that I am, I'm miserable and wonder now some women manage to have baby after baby! My poor husband has already succumbed to the idea that this might truly be our only child. My family and friends miss the old me; I miss the old me! The doctors and nurses keep telling me this stage will end soon, but these days seem never-ending. I wake up and dry heave, I eat and throw it up, then I dry heave some more and the cycle continues through my work day, and all the way until I get to bed.

Just what does "anything" look like though?

For many women, it looks suspiciously like pot. Marijuana. Cannabis. Because it is.

As one woman commented on the web site Momlogic .com, on a blog post about pregnancy,

> "During my first pregnancy, I was hospitalized repeatedly for dehydration due to severe hyperemesis," wrote Holly. "Zofran didn't work. I was so sick that I told my husband it was a good thing we didn't own a gun—and at that point, I wasn't kidding. . . . Did I eventually break down and try marijuana? You bet. Did it work? Yes. Do I feel guilty about it? Not a single bit."

Zofran vs. Marijuana

The drug to which she refers, Zofran, is a prescription drug recommended by some OB-GYNs and midwives to treat nausea in pregnant women. It was originally created for use by chemotherapy patients who suffer from extreme nausea and vomiting especially evident in the aforementioned hyperemesis gravidarum condition. It's true that Zofran works for some women; and, like with Holly, not at all for others. Some women question the safety of the medication, as well. Phenergan is another prescription medication to treat nausea and vomiting. These medications, however, are far from fail safe. Many women find themselves continuing to battle extreme dehydration and malnutrition and are desperate for relief—even if that relief comes in the form of an illegal drug. Erin Hildebrandt chronicled her experience with life-threatening vomiting and nausea in her five pregnancies in *Mothering* magazine and the remedy which finally "saved her,"

> " . . . as the nausea and vomiting increased, I began to lose weight. I was diagnosed as having hyperemesis gravidarum, a severe and constant form of morning sickness. I started researching the condition, desperately searching for a solution. I tried wristbands, herbs, yoga, pharmaceuticals, meditation—everything I could think of. Ultimately, after losing 20 pounds in the middle of pregnancy, and being hospitalized repeatedly for dehydration and migraines, I developed preeclampsia [a severe condition in late pregnancy] and was told an emergency cesarean [section] was necessary. . . .

> "In my second pregnancy . . . ten weeks after my first dose [of marijuana], I had gained 17 pounds over my pre-pregnant weight. I gave beautiful and joyous birth to a 9 pound, 2 ounce baby boy in the bed in which he'd been conceived. I know that using marijuana saved us both from many of the terrible dangers associated with malnutrition in pregnancy."

Marijuana is the most widely used illicit drug, by women of childbearing age in the United States, and it deserves more than a "talk to the hand" from health care providers, legal experts and advocates. It warrants what Lynn [M.] Paltrow of the National Advocates for Pregnant Women (NAPW) calls an "actual adult conversation" about the way pregnant women use marijuana for medicinal purposes—and the political and legal systems' move to prosecute pregnant women who may have used marijuana to quell nausea or treat extreme medical conditions.

The use of marijuana—or cannabis—to treat medical conditions is nothing new. Cannabis has been used for thousands of years for medicinal, spiritual and recreational purposes. In 2008, cannabis was found stashed in the tomb of a Chinese shaman from 2700 years ago. Experts hypothesized that it may have been used for medicinal purposes—possibly for pain relief.

Cannabis has also been used throughout ancient history to specifically treat women's reproductive health conditions—from menstrual cramps to the pain of childbirth. In the book *Women and Cannabis: Medicine, Science and Sociology* by Drs. Ethan Russo and Melanie Dreher and [Mary Lynn Mathre]:

> "Cannabis has an ancient tradition of usage as a medicine in obstetrics and gynecology ... but will surprise most by its depth of usage." The authors cite, as one example, the Ancient Egyptian mixture of hemp seeds with agents found in beer, to ease the pain of a "difficult chilbirth."

In this day and age, however, marijuana carries with it a heavy reputation. It is, of course, illegal.

Anti-Drug and Anti-Choice

After more than a century of state and legislative attention to the drug, including a governmental propaganda campaign in the early part of the twentieth century (*Reefer Madness* anyone?), marijuana is placed on par with all other illegal drugs including crack, cocaine and heroin. In the 1980s, thanks to then president Ronald Reagan, unprecedented criminal penalties for possession and dealing of marijuana were instituted and the "three strikes you're out" policy has given rise to an exponential increase in the number of Americans who have been arrested for possession of marijuana. Since then, however, a growing medical marijuana movement has emerged, successfully passing laws which legalize the use of marijuana for medicinal purposes, to varying degrees, in 15 states so far [as of December 2010].

We've arrived at a point in time where the intersection of strident—and extremely ineffective—drug policy has combined forces, however informally, with an equally strident anti-choice movement which has slowly helped to pass laws which criminalize pregnant women's behavior based on ideology and flimsy medical evidence. In Texas, the "Prenatal Protection Act" considers an embryo or fetus an "unborn child from conception to birth" for the purposes of murder or aggravated assault against a pregnant woman. It means an attacker can be considered for two crimes: one against the pregnant woman and one against her embryo or fetus. But pair that with drug laws like Texas's "Delivery of a Controlled Substance to a Minor," for example, and you have the perfect marriage of propaganda and control.

Alma Baker delivered twins in 2004 and tested positive for marijuana. She admitted that she smoked marijuana to treat nausea and increase her appetite during her pregnancy. Despite the fact that her children were healthy and developmentally advanced, the Texas D.A. [district attorney] in the county in which Baker lived brought charges against her based on both laws. Baker was placed on probation and fined. Her lawyer had this to say of Baker's felony prosecution:

> "This is an end around *Roe v. Wade*," he says, "and not a subtle one. By extension, where will we go with this? How about charging obese women or women who smoke with Child Endangerment?"

But, notes Lynn [M.] Paltrow, executive director for the National [Advocates] for Pregnant Women, the more urgent matter may be that these sorts of laws actually discourage pregnant women from seeking care. Alma Baker was clear:

> "If I would have known that I'd get in trouble for telling my doctor the truth I would have either lied or not gone to the doctor," she says.

Most major medical groups including the American Congress of Obstetricians and Gynecologists, the American Medical Association—and an increasing number of experts—agree with Paltrow. Paltrow's work over many years, providing extensive, evidence-based legal arguments against the prosecution of pregnant women for drug use, is consistently solidified by *medical* expert evidence and testimony on the effects of prosecuting pregnant women for prenatal marijuana use. But what about medical evidence on the actual, physiological effects of prenatal marijuana exposure on babies?

That's the problem. There isn't much of it.

Medical Evidence

The medical evidence is sparse given testing and trials involving pregnant women and illegal drug use are not exactly easy to undertake. So organizations and providers obviously tend towards relying on a more conservative framework when discussing which drugs and medications pregnant women can safely use. They also rely on information which seems to lump together women who abuse drugs, with women who may be using marijuana for truly medicinal purposes. Even the March of Dimes website cannot help but use the limited research on prenatal exposure to marijuana to craft a rather vague informational section on marijuana use during pregnancy:

> Some studies suggest that use of marijuana during pregnancy may slow fetal growth and slightly decrease the length of pregnancy (possibly increasing the risk of premature

Punishing Pregnant Women

For more than a decade, law enforcement personnel, judges, and elected officials nationwide have sought to punish women for their actions during pregnancy that may affect the fetuses they are carrying. Women who are having children despite substance abuse problems have been a particular target, finding themselves prosecuted for such nonexistent crimes as "fetal abuse" and delivery of drugs through the umbilical cord. In addition, pregnant women are being civilly committed or jailed, and new mothers are losing custody of their children even when they would be capable parents. Meanwhile, state legislators have repeatedly introduced substance abuse and child welfare proposals that would penalize only pregnant women with addiction problems.

Some proponents of these efforts are motivated by the misguided belief that they are promoting fetal health and protecting children. Others hope to gain legal recognition of "fetal rights"—the premise that a fetus has separate interests that are equal to or greater than those of a pregnant woman. Recognition of such rights would require women to subordinate their lives and health—including decisions about reproduction, medical care, and employment—to the fetus. In fact, doctors and hospital officials have already relied on this theory to seek court orders to force pregnant women to undergo cesarean sections or other medical procedures for the alleged benefit of the fetus.

Lynn M. Paltrow,
"Punishing Women for Their Behavior During Pregnancy:
An Approach That Undermines the Health of
Women and Children," National Advocates for Pregnant Women,
January 13, 2006. http://advocatesforpregnantwomen.org.

birth). These effects are seen mainly in women who use marijuana regularly (six or more times a week).

In one of the larger studies on prenatal marijuana exposure, published in the journal *Pediatrics* in 1994, Melanie Dreher, PhD, along with two of her colleagues, undertook an ethnographic study in Jamaica. The research focused on neonatal outcomes from the mothers' marijuana use during pregnancy. Results did not show any differences, at 3 days old and at one month old, between newborns exposed to marijuana in utero and those who hadn't been exposed. Why, Jamaica? From the report,

> With regard to the research context, it should be noted that virtually all the studies of prenatal exposure have been conducted in the United States and Canada where marijuana use is primarily recreational. This is in marked contrast to other societies, such as Jamaica, where scientific reports have documented the cultural integration of marijuana and its ritual and medicinal as well as recreational functions. *Previous studies have had difficulty controlling possible confounding effects of factors such as polydrug use, antenatal care, mothers' nutritional status, maternal age, SES and social support, as well as the effects of different caretaking environments, which could lead to differences in neonate behavior. The legal and social sanctions associated with illicit drug use often compromise self-report data and render it almost impossible to obtain accurate prenatal exposure levels.* [emphasis added]

In a study carried out in Canada, "Survey of Medicinal Cannabis Use Among Childbearing Women," researchers looked specifically at how 84 women who used marijuana during pregnancy to treat nausea, vomiting and hyperemesis gravidarum rated the effectiveness of "cannabis therapy." The women were recruited through "compassion societies"—where they receive medical marijuana. The authors found that almost all of the women—92 percent—found cannabis to be "extremely effective" or "effective" for treating nausea and vomiting and suggested that the use of marijuana to treat "severe nausea and vomiting" certainly warranted further investigation.

The evidence may be minimal but some physicians and midwives are suggesting marijuana use for extreme vomiting and nausea during pregnancy—regardless of the state of criminalization. One midwife I spoke with, who preferred that I do not use her name, told me:

> "I do encourage moms to use marijuana *in moderation and only as needed for extreme nausea and vomiting in early pregnancy*. I also tell them that marijuana has an estrogenic effect and that overuse could theoretically disrupt early pregnancy hormones and place someone at risk for miscarriage, but it's not likely."

On Momlogic.com, women share stories of their physicians suggesting marijuana use as well. Writing of her horrific experience with vomiting and nausea during pregnancy, Jessica Katz wrote:

> Even though I am taking Zofran again, I am deathly ill. Now, I know that while you're pregnant you are supposed to limit caffeine, stop eating sushi and nitrates and not even touch Excedrin. So you can imagine my surprise when my doctor suggested marijuana as a treatment for morning sickness. I was floored. I am pretty sure that you are not supposed to do drugs in general, let alone when you are carrying a child. Don't they take your kids away from you if you do drugs while you are pregnant?
>
> I went home and Googled this remedy. Could it be real? I found page after page of moms saying they'd used medical marijuana to treat their severe morning sickness, and that it had worked.

Other pregnant women on the site rushed to tell her she wasn't alone:

> "If I [hadn't smoked] marijuana when I was pregnant with my second child, I would have never eaten," wrote Anony-

mous. "The smell [and] taste of food made me so sick I couldn't stand it. I didn't do much—just a small hit, and then I was fine. If [your doctor] said it will help, believe him."

Women vs. Experts

On Babycenter.com, when one of their "pregnancy experts" dared to suggest that marijuana use during pregnancy was shown to be unsafe through studies, and equated it with smoking tobacco, currently and formerly pregnant women rose up, to dispute his claims:

> I SUFFERED FROM THROWING UP, NOT BEING ABLE TO DIGEST ANY FOOD AND EVERYTHING ELSE ASSOCIATED W/ MORNING SICKNESS & THE ONLY THING THAT RELIEVED ME FROM IT WAS IF I SMOKED A LITTLE WEED.

> I am a toxicologist, and nothing saddens me more than patronizing "professionals" . . . who present unsubstantiated speculations as facts. It is far too easy in this society to scare women with such misinformation. . . .

> My message to . . . the world is to stop patronizing women and admit that it is HIGHLY likely given the generations of people born to women who smoked marijuana (or had a couple beers for pete's sake!) during pregnancy, that this is not a "drug" worth demonizing.

But when pregnant women do resort to utilizing cannabis to treat extreme vomiting, appetite problems and malnutrition, they may be placing themselves in danger—not only in terms of the criminalization of possession in states where medical marijuana is not legal. They are leaving themselves open to being drug tested after their baby is born and then potentially prosecuted for child abuse and neglect. It's the "Alma Baker" scenario mentioned above. Says the midwife with whom I spoke:

"I counsel women that if there is a hospital transfer and the hospital conducts a drug test that she *could* be placing herself and her baby at risk of some unwanted intervention."

In states where medical marijuana laws apply, pregnant women are allowed to use marijuana to treat pregnancy related symptoms. Sabrina Fendrick of NORML (National Organization for the Reform of Marijuana Laws) Women's Alliance told RH Reality Check that just because a pregnant woman is allowed to access marijuana for medicinal purposes in those states where it's legal, it doesn't necessarily mean that she'll be automatically protected when it comes to drug testing, however. And in those states where marijuana use is illegal, Fendrick says she receives e-mails "at least once a week" from mothers who are in danger of losing their children after having tested positive for marijuana use after giving birth.

In South Carolina in 2009, a mother who had used marijuana during pregnancy was prosecuted for child abuse and no less than three medical experts came to her defense to decry the lack of any evidence of physiological, emotional or mental effects from the marijuana use. Dr. Deborah Frank, Harvard educated, board certified in pediatrics, and a professor of pediatrics at Boston University School of Medicine not only found no evidence of abuse but said the child "appeared to be doing very well" and was developing in a positive way. Dr. Peter Fried, a PhD in psychology and a retired professor from Carleton University in Ottawa, Canada, has done extensive research on prenatal exposure to marijuana. Though he's found some potentially negative effects, in this case, he stated clearly that "to characterize an infant born to a woman who used marijuana during pregnancy as 'physically abused' and/or neglected is contrary to all scientific evidence. The use of marijuana during pregnancy has not been shown by any objective research to result in abuse or neglect."

Prioritize the Mother and Child

This isn't a question of whether or not marijuana can be used as a medicinal for particular, chronic, extreme conditions during pregnancy. Pregnant woman around the world are already doing what they need to—to keep themselves happy and to keep their fetuses growing and healthy. Physicians and midwives recognize the medicinal properties and prescribe the use of marijuana in certain cases as well. Citizens are fighting to pass laws which do the same. Reproductive justice advocates may be understandably nervous about a potential alliance with advocates who work on drug policy issues. Considering anti-choice politics make it next to impossible to engage in an evidence-based discussion on the risks vs. benefits of medicinal marijuana in pregnancy, it's extraordinarily difficult to have the "adult conversation" advocates like Lynn Paltrow work so hard to sustain. Laws that serve only to control the lives of pregnant and parenting women, at the expense of both women's and children's health and safety, are born from anti-choice legislators and advocates. In the now, we have pregnant women in this country that are either forced to turn to illegal drugs in order to experience relief from, at times, a life-threatening condition or find themselves embroiled in a legal system which seems to prioritize laws in the abstract over what's truly in the best interest of mother and child.

> "Recent well-conducted studies suggest
> [marijuana] might have subtle nega-
> tive effects on neurobehavioural out-
> comes."

Marijuana Use
During Pregnancy May
Have Adverse Outcomes

Eran Kozer and Gideon Koren

*Eran Kozer is a doctor with pediatric emergency services at Tel
Aviv University; Gideon Koren is a professor of pediatrics at the
University of Western Ontario. In the following viewpoint, the
authors report that studies on marijuana use have been inconclusive. However, they argue that evidence suggests that marijuana use during pregnancy causes some subtle long-term problems for children, such as sleep disturbances and hyperactivity.*

As you read, consider the following questions:

1. Why do the authors say that assessing the outcome of in
   utero exposure to marijuana is complex?

2. What have studies shown about the relationship between marijuana use during pregnancy and birth weight, according to the authors?

3. Why do the authors say there could be an important influence on public health even if marijuana has only a small influence on neurobehavioral outcomes?

Question: I am treating a 27-year-old woman who is now in her 10th week of pregnancy. She smokes marijuana two to three times a week, but does not use other drugs. She also smokes 20 cigarettes a day. I am concerned about the effects of marijuana exposure on her baby.

Answer: It is not always possible to isolate the effect of marijuana exposure from other possible confounders on pregnancy outcome. Although marijuana is not an established human teratogen [a chemical that disturbs fetal development], recent well-conducted studies suggest it might have subtle negative effects on neurobehavioural outcomes, including sleep disturbances, impaired visual problem solving, hyperactivity, impassivity, inattention, and increased delinquency.

Marijuana is a drug prepared from the plant *Cannabis sativa*. It contains more than 400 chemicals including tetrahydrocannabinol (THC), its psychoactive component, which is rapidly absorbed from the lungs into the bloodstream and is metabolized primarily by the liver. Prolonged fetal exposure can occur if the mother is a regular user because THC crosses the placenta and because detectable levels can be found in various tissues up to 30 days after a single use.

Trying to assess the outcome of in utero exposure to marijuana is complex. In many of the studies on marijuana exposure and pregnancy outcome, women who consume marijuana also smoked tobacco, drank alcohol, or used other drugs. The effect of marijuana exposure cannot always be isolated from other possible confounders. These limitations should be kept in mind when prenatal exposure to marijuana is considered.

Effects on a Fetus

Birth weight. Several studies demonstrated a small reduction in birth weight associated with use of marijuana during pregnancy, while others failed to show such an effect. A recent meta-analysis combined the results from 10 different studies on maternal cannabis use and birth weight and showed only weak association between maternal cannabis use and birth weight. The largest reduction in mean birth weight for any cannabis use was 48 g [grams]. Cannabis use at least four times a day was associated with a larger reduction of 131 g in mean birth weight. The authors concluded that there is inadequate evidence that cannabis, at the amount typically consumed by pregnant women, causes low birth weight.

Teratogenicity. Marijuana has not been implicated as a human teratogen. No homogeneous pattern of malformation has been observed that could be considered characteristic of intrauterine marijuana exposure. Among 202 infants exposed to marijuana prenatally, the rate of serious malformations was no higher than the rate among infants whose mothers did not use marijuana.

Postnatal mortality. The mortality rate during the first 2 years of life was determined in 2964 infants. About 44% of the infants tested positive for drugs: 30.5% tested positive for cocaine, 20.2% for opiates, and 11.4% for cannabinoids. Mortality rates among the cannabinoid-positive group and the drug-negative group were not significantly different.

Risk of childhood malignancy. A case-control study assessed in utero and postnatal exposures to drugs in 204 children with acute nonlymphoblastic leukemia. An 11-fold risk was found for maternal use of marijuana just before or during pregnancy. These findings should be interpreted cautiously because the rate of marijuana exposure in the control group was less than 1%. This rate is much lower than the 9% to 27% rate reported by others, and might represent recall or reporting bias in this group. Such bias could increase the odds ratio

(OR) associated with the exposure. In addition to the limitations of this study, another study could not confirm such an association.

Another case-control study found an increased risk for rhabdomyosarcoma [a malignant tumor of the muscles] among children exposed to marijuana in utero. In this study, it was impossible to differentiate between the effects of other agents on outcome because many women consumed marijuana with other drugs.

Current data are inconclusive, and further studies are needed to determine whether childhood malignancy is a true risk for fetuses exposed to marijuana.

Neurodevelopmental Effects

Short- and long-term neurodevelopmental effects of prenatal exposure to marijuana are not clear. Because many women who use marijuana during pregnancy also use other illicit drugs, there are methodologic difficulties in interpreting the effects. In many studies, it is also difficult to isolate the effect of marijuana from other confounders, such as socioeconomic status, family structure, and mother's personality. Despite these limitations, evidence suggests that marijuana exposure during pregnancy has adverse fetal effects.

Sleep disturbances at 3 years of age were more common among offspring of women who used marijuana during pregnancy compared with controls. The two groups were similar in maternal age, race, income, education, and maternal use of alcohol, nicotine, and other substances during the first trimester.

Child behavior was assessed at 10 years of age in 635 children from low-income families. Prenatal exposure to marijuana was associated with hyperactivity, impassivity, inattention, and increased delinquency. In this cohort, women who used marijuana differed significantly from those who did not in many confounders that could affect child development. Al-

Marijuana and Fetal Growth

Objective: Cannabis is the most commonly consumed illicit drug among pregnant women. Intrauterine exposure to cannabis may result in risks for the developing fetus. The importance of intrauterine growth on subsequent psychological and behavioral child development has been demonstrated. This study examined the relation between maternal cannabis use and fetal growth until birth in a population-based sample.

Method: Approximately 7,452 mothers enrolled during pregnancy and provided information on substance use and fetal growth. Fetal growth was determined using ultrasound measures in early, mid, and late pregnancy. Additionally, birth weight was assessed.

Results: Maternal cannabis use during pregnancy was associated with growth restriction in mid and late pregnancy and with lower birth weight. This growth reduction was most pronounced for fetuses exposed to continued maternal cannabis use during pregnancy. Fetal weight in cannabis-exposed fetuses showed a growth reduction of -14.44 g [grams]/week and head circumference, compared with non-exposed fetuses. Maternal cannabis use during pregnancy resulted in more pronounced growth restriction than maternal tobacco use. Paternal cannabis use was not associated with fetal growth restriction.

Conclusions:: Maternal cannabis use, even for a short period, may be associated with several adverse fetal growth trajectories.

Hanan El Marroun et al.,
"Intrauterine Cannabis Exposure Affects Fetal Growth Trajectories:
The Generation R Study," Journal of the American Academy
of Child & Adolescent Psychiatry, *December 2009.*

though investigators tried to control for these variables, differences in behavior might be partially explained by other unrecognized confounders. In another study of one hundred forty six 9- to 12-year-old children, prenatal exposure to marijuana was not associated with intelligence, memory, or attention deficits. The study showed prenatal exposure to marijuana is associated with poorer visual problem solving.

An example of the difficulties associated with assessing neurobehavioural outcomes after in utero exposure to marijuana comes from Jamaica. A study was conducted in an area where marijuana use is very common, and women who use large doses of marijuana are better educated and more independent than women who consume small doses of marijuana. At the age of 1 month, infants of heavy marijuana-using mothers had better scores on autonomic stability, quality of alertness, irritability, and self-regulation and were judged to be more rewarding for caregivers. The authors suggested that these differences related to the characteristics of the mothers using marijuana.

It is possible, though, that neurobehavioural effects associated with in utero exposure to marijuana, which were observed in studies conducted in Western countries, are partially related to the socioeconomic, behavioral, and psychological characteristics of women who consume marijuana during pregnancy and not to the exposure itself.

Marijuana is probably the most common illicit drug used during pregnancy. Taking into account the large number of infants with prenatal exposure to marijuana, even a small influence on neurobehavioural parameters could have a noticeable effect on public health.

Marijuana and Breastfeeding

Tetrahydrocannabinol [THC] is transferred into breast milk and levels can be up to eight times higher than in the mother's bloodstream. Exposure to marijuana through breast milk might delay infants' motor development. The American Academy of Pediatrics considers use of marijuana as a contraindication for breastfeeding. It is advisable to abstain from all use of THC while breastfeeding.

> *"Are you for symptom relief or getting stoned? That used to be a fuzzy question. Now it's concrete."*

It Is Possible to Get the Medical Benefits of Marijuana Without the High

William Saletan

William Saletan is the national correspondent at Slate.com. In the following viewpoint, he discusses Sativex, a new drug that is basically a refined and standardized version of marijuana. Saletan notes that Sativex specifically attempts to provide the therapeutic effects of marijuana without the high associated with the drug. He concludes that such products should force both the political left and right to have a more serious discussion focused on using marijuana for symptom relief rather than for getting stoned.

As you read, consider the following questions:

1. Why does Saletan suggest his readers might be snickering about Sativex?

2. What does Saletan say are some of the problems with allowing everyone to grow and smoke their own marijuana?

3. According to Saletan, what are the side effects of Marinol and Cesamet?

We've taken the caffeine out of coffee, the alcohol out of beer, and the smoke out of tobacco. What's next?

Taking the fun out of pot.

Sativex Isn't Pot

GW Pharmaceuticals, a British company, has just requested European approval of Sativex, a "cannabinoid pharmaceutical product."

What's that? Do I hear you snickering at your keyboard? You think this is a backdoor way of legalizing weed?

For shame, says the company:

> Sativex is a cannabinoid pharmaceutical product standardized in composition, formulation, and dose, administered by means of an appropriate delivery system, which has been, and continues to be, tested in properly controlled preclinical and clinical studies. Crude herbal cannabis in any form—including a crude extract or tincture—is none of those things.

So there. Sativex isn't pot. It's a carefully refined derivative: "Once the plants have matured, they are harvested and dried. GW then extracts the cannabinoids and other pharmacologically active components . . . [to] arrive at a pharmaceutical grade material." Patients are further expected to regulate their intake to separate pot's approved effects—relief of pain and spasms—from its unapproved effects:

> By careful self-titration (dose adjustment), most patients are able to separate the thresholds for symptom relief and in-

toxication, the 'therapeutic window', so enabling them to obtain symptom relief without experiencing a 'high'.

Bummer, eh? The company knows exactly what you're thinking:

Why not just let patients smoke cannabis?

> In GW's opinion, smoking is not an acceptable means of delivery for a medicine. We believe that patients wish to use a medicine that is legally prescribed, does not require smoking, is of guaranteed quality, has been developed and approved by regulatory authorities for use in their specific medical condition and is dispensed by pharmacists under the supervision of their doctor.

That's a sensible approach. From the standpoint of medicinal as opposed to recreational use, it certainly makes more sense than letting everybody grow and smoke the herb, with all the resulting variability, fraud, and side effects. But GW's anti-pot evangelism goes further:

> GW has never endorsed or supported the idea of distributing or legalizing crude herbal cannabis for medical use. In both our publications and presentations, we have consistently maintained that only a cannabinoid medication—one that is standardized in composition, formulation, and dose, administered by means of an appropriate delivery system, and tested in properly controlled preclinical and clinical studies—can meet the standards of regulatory authorities around the world, including those of the FDA [US Food and Drug Administration].

And don't even think of breaking in and stealing the raw goods:

> GW's cannabis plants are grown under computer-controlled conditions in secure glasshouses at a secret location in the UK. . . . The facility is situated in the South of England but for clear security reasons we do not divulge the precise location.

Sativex vs. Marinol

Sativex differs from Marinol in important ways. First, it incorporates CBD [cannabidiol] and other plant ingredients as well as THC [the active ingredient in marijuana]. GW [the company that produces Sativex] says that its research showed the mixture is more effective, partly because CBD mitigated untoward psychoactive effects of pure THC. Sativex was first developed for treating symptoms of MS [multiple sclerosis], but is also being tested for neuropathic pain from spinal cord injury, cancer, and diabetes. GW is also developing a higher-CBD product for rheumatoid arthritis, inflammatory bowel diseases, epilepsy and psychotic disorders, and a high-THC product for chronic pain.

Second, Sativex is not a pill, but a spray delivered under the tongue. This delivery method is not as fast as inhalation, as it still takes several minutes for the cannabinoids to be absorbed through the membranes of the mouth. However, it is faster than oral ingestion. It also delivers a far more consistent dosage, since the cannabinoids are absorbed directly into the blood from the oral membranes without having to pass through the digestive system.

Third, Sativex is cheaper to manufacture because the cannabinoids are derived from the plant rather than expensive chemical synthesis.

Dale Gieringer, Ed Rosenthal,
and Gregory T. Carter,
Marijuana Medical Handbook:
Practical Guide to Therapeutic Uses of Marijuana.
Oakland, CA: Quick American, 2008.

Symptom Relief vs. Getting Stoned

In your wildest dreams, did you imagine that a recreational drug could be so thoroughly, piously sterilized? But here it is. First came Cesamet (a "synthetic cannabinoid"), then Marinol (also synthetic). Only one pesky side effect has remained: Cesamet produces "euphoria in the recommended dosage range," and Marinol causes "easy laughing" and "elation." We can't have that. So the quest to "separate the thresholds for symptom relief and intoxication" continues. According to GW, delivery of Sativex as a spray "enables patients to titrate (adjust) their dose to achieve symptom relief without incurring an unacceptable degree of side effects."

All of which underscores Human Nature's basic question about the war on drugs. Namely: What do you mean by drugs? A war on cigarettes or on nicotine? A war on caffeinated but not alcoholic beer? Legalization of "cannabinoid medication" but not cannabis?

Drugs can be, and are being, re-engineered every day. Nicotine and caffeine appear in new forms. Cannabis is an herb, then a powder, then a capsule, and now a spray, with significant chemical adjustments along the way. (Update, May 28 [2009]: The Marijuana Policy Project argues that the spray formulation has already been eclipsed by a better way to filter and deliver the drug's therapeutic benefits: vapor.) How do you fight an enemy that keeps changing? How do you recognize when it's no longer your enemy?

Every feat of re-engineering challenges our moral and legal assumptions. In the case of Sativex, two positions are under attack: the Left's lazy tolerance of recreational marijuana in the guise of legalizing medical marijuana and the Right's opposition to medical marijuana on the grounds that it's just a pretext. By refining, isolating, and standardizing pot's medicinal effects, pharmaceutical companies are showing us how to separate the two uses. Are you for symptom relief or getting stoned? That used to be a fuzzy question. Now it's concrete: Do you want the reefer or the spray?

| "Take away the psychoactive stimulant properties and most people will experience significantly less relief. The 'high' is part and parcel of the restorative powers of cannabis."

The High Is Part of the Medical Benefit of Marijuana

Lanny Swerdlow

Lanny Swerdlow is a registered nurse and a medical marijuana activist. In the following viewpoint, he argues that the marijuana high is part of the beneficial effect of the drug. He says that separating the high and the medicinal benefits of the drug is difficult and often has dangerous side effects. He adds that many people taking marijuana for medicinal purposes feel sick and that the high helps them relax and gives them pleasure. He concludes that the effort to eliminate the marijuana high is a waste of time and resources.

As you read, consider the following questions:

1. What does Swerdlow say were the negative side effects of Rimonabant?

2. Why does Swerdlow think it is suspicious that NIAAA is conducting research on marijuana?

3. According to Swerdlow, in what way can cancer patients benefit from marijuana?

The objection to marijuana as medicine has always centered on the psychoactive effects of this ancient herb. The mantra is "if only we could develop marijuana that would relieve pain, facilitate sleep and stem nausea and do it without the 'high,' then we would have the best of both worlds."

Removing Pleasure

The hope for marijuana as medicine without the high nirvana got a boost in April [2011] when Dr. Li Zhang of the U.S. National Institute on Alcohol Abuse and Alcoholism [NIAAA] reported his team had discovered that the psychoactive effects of marijuana can be "decoupled" from its pain-alleviating properties.

THC [tetrahydrocannabinol, the active ingredient in marijuana] gives people a "high" by binding to a molecular anchor on cells called the cannabinoid type-1 (CB1) receptor. Zhang discovered that THC relieves pain by binding to the receptors for the neurotransmitter glycine. If you can block the CB1 receptors but leave the pain relieving glycine receptors available, then you can relieve pain without any psychoactive stimulation.

How do you block the CB1 receptors? According to the April 2011 issue of *New Scientist*, it's done with another drug.

Of course monkeying around with the cannabinoid system is risky business as vividly demonstrated by the weight loss drug Rimonabant which worked by blocking CB1 receptor sites. By blocking the CB1 receptor sites, Rimonabant should diminish appetite and people would eat less and lose weight.

Along with weight loss, however, came a significant increase in anxiety, depression and suicidal thoughts. The drug was pulled from the market.

But if we can take the pleasure and enjoyment out of using cannabis, then the folks at NIAAA see developing anxiety, depression and suicidal thoughts as an acceptable trade-off for not getting "the high."

More to the point is why NIAAA is conducting a study on eliminating the marijuana high in the first place. It is highly suspicious considering that their mission statement is to provide "leadership in the national effort to reduce alcohol-related problems" followed by a list of categories all related to alcohol—none to marijuana or any other drug. Considering that NIAAA is funding this study, someone might have reasonably asked Dr. Zhang why he was working on eliminating the high in marijuana and not alcohol.

NIAAA's study on how to eliminate the cannabis high becomes even more absurd as it is the "high" that successfully helps alcoholics abstain from drinking alcohol, turn their lives around and become productive and healthy members of the community. It would seem that NIAAA should be studying how to enhance that property of marijuana rather than how to eliminate it.

No High Is Not a Benefit

I have encountered a few medical marijuana patients who specifically seek out strains that produce little or no high. However, the vast majority of patients seek out strains that give them a psychoactive stimulant, "the high," while at the same time relieving their pain, anxiety, depression, glaucoma or whatever debilitating symptoms they are consuming cannabis to mitigate.

Take away the psychoactive stimulant properties and most people will experience significantly less relief. The "high" is part and parcel of the restorative powers of cannabis.

John Cox and Allen Forkum, "Doobious," Cox & Forkum; June 7, 2005. www.coxand forkum.com. Copyright © 2005 by Cox & Forkum. Reproduced by permission.

Unbelievably, there are other studies like Dr. Zhang's being funded. Dr. Keun-Hang Susan Yang has written about her research into decoupling the "high" from the CBDs [cannabidiols]. These cannabinoids help prevent nausea and are highly beneficial to cancer patients undergoing cancer chemotherapy. Does Dr. Yang really believe that the vast majority of cancer patients use cannabis solely to control their nausea?

Don't they get it? These people feel awful—they have CANCER and there are other horrors going on in their lives as a result of that diagnosis. Isn't it wonderful that marijuana can help stem the nausea and at the same time treat their depression and just make them "feel better"? For what possible reason would you want to "decouple the high" in most cancer patients?

Why is this nation spending its scarce research dollars trying to "decouple the high" while there is hardly a dime going into research on the incredible, mind-boggling and astounding anticancer efficacy of cannabis. It's 21st-century *Reefer Madness* [referring to a hyperbolic 1936 film about the evils of marijuana].

Periodical and Internet Sources Bibliography

The following articles have been selected to supplement the diverse views presented in this chapter.

Kathleen Doheny	"Marijuana Relieves Chronic Pain, Research Shows," *WebMD*, August 30, 2010. www.webmd.com.
Katie Drummond	"Tripping on Wombs: Cannabis for Pregnancy Nausea?," *True/Slant*, November 4, 2009. http://trueslant.com.
FOX News	"Study: Too Much Marijuana Makes Pain Worse, Not Better," October 24, 2007. www.foxnews.com.
Huffington Post	"Marijuana Provides Pain Relief, New Study Says," April 20, 2010. www.huffingtonpost.com.
Marie Myung-Ok Lee	"Why I Give My 9-Year-Old Pot," *Slate*, May 11, 2009.
Tiffany O'Callaghan	"Can Smoking Pot Lower Your Threshold for Pain?," *Time*, August 14, 2009.
Reuters	"Pot Smoking During Pregnancy May Stunt Fetal Growth," January 22, 2010. www.reuters.com.
Mark Robichaux	"Researchers Aim to Develop Marijuana Without the High," *Wall Street Journal*, February 28, 2001.
Nikki Ross	"Marijuana Treatment for Autism: A High Need for Research," *Nikki Rossi*, March 9, 2010. http://myportfolio.usc.edu.
The Week	"Marijuana Without the High: A Painkiller Breakthrough," April 5, 2011.

Should Medical Marijuana Be Legalized?

Chapter Preface

The medical use of marijuana is an ongoing source of controversy. Many doctors, researchers, and state governments argue that marijuana does have useful medical applications. However, the federal government has consistently argued that marijuana has no medical function.

On June 21, 2011, the US Drug Enforcement Administration (DEA) finally ruled on a nine-year-old petition asking the agency to recategorize marijuana, dropping it from the schedule I list of the most dangerous controlled substances. The DEA responded to the petition by stating the following:

> After gathering the necessary data, DEA requested a scientific and medical evaluation and scheduling recommendation from the Department of Health and Human Services (DHHS). DHHS concluded that marijuana has a high potential for abuse, has no accepted medical use in the United States, and lacks an acceptable level of safety for use even under medical supervision. Therefore, DHHS recommended that marijuana remain in schedule I.

The DEA added specifically in reference to medical use of marijuana that:

> Marijuana does not have a currently accepted medical use in treatment in the United States or a currently accepted medical use with severe restrictions. The Center for Medicinal Cannabis Research in California, among others, is conducting research with marijuana at the IND [investigational new drug] level, but these studies have not yet progressed to the stage of submitting an NDA [new drug application]. Thus, at this time, the known risks of marijuana use have not been shown to be outweighed by specific benefits in well-controlled clinical trials that scientifically evaluate safety and efficacy.

A number of commentators disputed the DEA's finding. Maia Szalavitz, writing at *Time* magazine's *Healthland* blog on July 11, 2011, argued that the DEA was basing its opinions on politics rather than science. Szalavitz said that evidence of marijuana's use for many conditions has been mounting. For example, Szalavitz argued that cannabinoids such as marijuana "have been found to help kill breast cancer cells, fight liver cancer, reduce inflammation, have antipsychotic effects and even potentially help stave off the development of Alzheimer's disease and reduce progression of Huntington's disease."

According to Jan Werner, the vice president of the Clearview Lake Corp., which runs marijuana collectives in California, "The bigger picture is by doing that [keeping marijuana as schedule I] they're keeping it in the same category as heroin and LSD, which are considered nonmedical value drugs. It keeps doctors from writing a normal prescription (to patients)," as quoted in a July 18, 2011, article in the *Contra Costa Times*.

Cannabis advocates plan to appeal the DEA decision in court, though a ruling may take years.

This chapter examines other debates surrounding the medical use of marijuana.

> *"Voter or legislative initiative does not meet the scientific standards for approval of medicine."*

The FDA's Opposition to Medical Marijuana Legalization Is Based on Science

Drug-Free Action Alliance and Alcohol and Drug Abuse Prevention Association of Ohio

Drug-Free Action Alliance is a nonprofit drug prevention agency. Alcohol and Drug Abuse Prevention Association of Ohio is a not-for-profit association that works to prevent the abuse of alcohol, tobacco, and drugs. In the following viewpoint, these organizations argue that marijuana should be evaluated for use in the same scientific manner as any other substance. The viewpoint states that at the moment evidence indicates that marijuana has no medical use. If new evidence becomes available, it says, the legality of marijuana can be evaluated. However, the organizations argue that marijuana should not be legalized through voter or legislative initiative, because such initiatives are not scientific.

As you read, consider the following questions:

1. What does a schedule I classification indicate, according to the viewpoint?

2. According to the viewpoint, what organizations have concluded that no scientific studies support medical use of marijuana?

3. According to the viewpoint, why may voter and legislative passage of marijuana-as-medicine laws inhibit good medicine?

Efforts to legalize marijuana as medicine in the United States have grown significantly in recent years. Approximately one-fourth of the states have passed legislation or ballot issues allowing marijuana to be prescribed within that state, though few have actually implemented these new policies. Marijuana remains a schedule I substance under federal law—a classification indicating it has no currently accepted medical use in the United States.

Medical Claims

There is some research that indicates marijuana may help decrease nausea, stimulate appetite, and decrease pain. The research is limited, and the Food and Drug Administration (FDA), along with most national medical associations—including the American Medical Association (AMA), American Academy of Pediatrics, National Institutes of Health, Institute of Medicine, American Cancer Society, National Cancer Institute and National Multiple Sclerosis Society—does not support smoked marijuana as medicine. However, the AMA has adopted a resolution calling for further clinical research into any therapeutic benefits of cannabinoid-based medicines. The AMA emphasizes that this resolution should not be viewed as endorsing the state marijuana-as-medicine programs.

Leading medical organizations note that safer treatment options exist. In addition, the FDA has approved a synthetic version of THC [tetrahydrocannabinol], the psychoactive ingredient in marijuana. Named Marinol, it is taken orally. It is a schedule II drug and is available by prescription in all 50 states.

Marijuana should be subject to the same research, consideration, and study as any other potential medicine. The U.S. Food and Drug Administration (FDA) is the sole federal agency that approves drug products as safe and effective for intended indications. The Federal Food, Drug, and Cosmetic (FD&C) Act requires that new drugs be shown to be safe and effective for their intended use before being marketed in this country. FDA's drug approval process requires well-controlled clinical trials that provide the necessary scientific data upon which FDA makes its approval and labeling decisions. If a drug product is to be marketed, then disciplined, systematic, scientifically conducted trials are the best means to obtain data to ensure that drug is safe and effective when used as indicated. Efforts that seek to bypass the FDA drug approval process would not serve the interests of public health because they might expose patients to unsafe and ineffective drug products. FDA has not approved smoked marijuana for any condition or disease indication.

Marijuana is listed in schedule I of the Controlled Substances Act (CSA), the most restrictive schedule. The Drug Enforcement Administration (DEA), which administers the CSA, continues to support that placement, and FDA concurred because marijuana met the three criteria for placement in schedule I under 21 U.S.C. 812(b)(1) (e.g., marijuana has a high potential for abuse, has no currently accepted medical use in treatment in the United States, and has a lack of accepted safety for use under medical supervision). Furthermore, there is currently sound evidence that smoked marijuana is harmful. A past evaluation by several Department of

Health and Human Services (HHS) agencies, including the Food and Drug Administration (FDA), Substance Abuse and Mental Health Services Administration (SAMHSA) and National Institute on Drug Abuse (NIDA), concluded that no sound scientific studies supported medical use of marijuana for treatment in the United States, and no animal or human data supported the safety or efficacy of marijuana for general medical use. There are alternative FDA-approved medications in existence for treatment of many of the proposed uses of smoked marijuana.

A growing number of states have passed voter referenda (or legislative actions) making smoked marijuana available for a variety of medical conditions upon a doctor's recommendation. These measures are inconsistent with efforts to ensure that medications undergo the rigorous scientific scrutiny of the FDA approval process and are proven safe and effective under the standards of the FD&C Act.

More Research Needed

There is already a substantial body of research demonstrating the health and safety risks from the use of marijuana. More research on marijuana, including possible medical applications as well as research on associated health and impairment risks from the use of marijuana, is needed. Not only is there a need for more research on any possible medical benefits, but also on identifying the chemicals within marijuana associated with any benefits, appropriate dosage levels, and safe means of administration, should medical benefits exist.

Voter or legislative initiative does not meet the scientific standards for approval of medicine. For example, we would not consider it rational to go to the polls to "vote on" a potential antibiotic. Voter and legislative passage of marijuana-as-medicine laws may actually inhibit good medicine because they shortcut the necessary step of researching the marijuana plant and the chemicals within that may have legitimate medi-

Marinol vs. Smoked Marijuana

Unlike smoked marijuana—which contains more than 400 different chemicals, including most of the hazardous chemicals found in tobacco smoke—Marinol has been studied and approved by the medical community and the Food and Drug Administration (FDA), the nation's watchdog over unsafe and harmful food and drug products. Since the passage of the 1906 Pure Food and Drug Act, any drug that is marketed in the United States must undergo rigorous scientific testing. The approval process mandated by this act ensures that claims of safety and therapeutic value are supported by clinical evidence and keeps unsafe, ineffective and dangerous drugs off the market.

There are no FDA-approved medications that are smoked. For one thing, smoking is generally a poor way to deliver medicine. It is difficult to administer safe, regulated dosages of medicines in smoked form. Secondly, the harmful chemicals and carcinogens that are by-products of smoking create entirely new health problems. There are four times the level of tar in a marijuana cigarette, for example, than in a tobacco cigarette.

"'Medical' Marijuana—The Facts,"
US Drug Enforcement Administration. www.justice.gov.

cal applications. Emotional testimony and personal opinion should not dictate medical treatment.

Consideration of marijuana as medicine should be treated with the same logical, rational approach as any other drug that has demonstrated health and safety risks yet may have some medical benefit: The medical and scientific community establishes policy based on available knowledge while continuing to conduct research on the drug to increase that knowledge base. Anything less puts the safety and health of the general public at risk.

Drug-Free Action Alliance and the Alcohol and Drug Abuse Prevention Association of Ohio (ADAPAO) do not support marijuana as medicine nor legislative or ballot initiatives to consider this policy change. Should future research result in the FDA changing position on marijuana as medicine, ADAPAO and Drug-Free Action Alliance would reconsider this position.

| "Virtually no research on potential risks and benefits has been done, because the government has blocked such studies."

The FDA's Opposition to Medical Marijuana Legalization Is Based on Politics

Sydney Spiesel

Sydney Spiesel is a pediatrician and a clinical professor of pediatrics at Yale University School of Medicine. In the following viewpoint, he reports that the Food and Drug Administration (FDA) has issued a statement declaring that marijuana has no safe medical uses. Spiesel says that this statement is not based on science. The best evidence, Spiesel argues, suggests that marijuana may have medical uses but that further study is needed. Spiesel contends, however, that the government has blocked marijuana research. He concludes that the FDA's statement is based on politics, and he calls into question the objectivity of government science.

As you read, consider the following questions:

1. What does Spiesel say the FDA's statement implies, and is this implication accurate?

2. What benefits did the IOM report suggest might result from medical marijuana use?

3. What other example of politics trumping science at the FDA does Spiesel provide?

L ast week [in April 2006], the Food and Drug Administration (FDA) reported that it had definitively established that marijuana has no medical use or value. Definitively? Established? I don't think so.

No New Analysis

The FDA's announcement begins by acknowledging the claim that smoked marijuana may be beneficial for some conditions. Then the agency points out that among drugs with a potential for abuse, marijuana is lumped in with the most dangerous drugs, the ones that have no potential medical benefits and the highest likelihood of misuse. The FDA next affirms that a collection of federal agencies have together concluded that marijuana is both dangerous and medically valueless, based on scientific studies in humans and animals. The announcement—actually, it's an "inter-agency advisory"—concludes by asserting, with a boldness that might belie a certain uneasiness, that it is the FDA's job to approve drugs. Take that, state legislatures and voters.

The FDA's statement implies that the agency reached its conclusion about marijuana after conducting a new serious analysis of the existing scientific literature on the drug. But of course no such analysis was reported in the medical literature and, in fact, no identifiable official at the FDA took responsibility for last week's advisory. It was just put out there as a statement of fact.

But it's not. In 1999, the Institute of Medicine [IOM], the medical arm of the National Academy of Sciences (an organization chartered by Congress to provide independent, nonpartisan scientific and technological advice) examined this same question in considerable depth and published a 288-page report of its findings. Put together by 11 distinguished scientists and physicians, the IOM report examined the known and potential harms of marijuana use and the known and potential medical benefits. The report is broad in its vision and thoughtful and cautious in its interpretations and recommendations. Its authors acknowledged that the medical uses of marijuana entail some risk of harm—for instance, it's pretty clear that inhaling marijuana smoke can't be good for the lungs, and who knows if there are significant psychological side effects for some users. But the authors concluded that these risks were not terribly high. They also found that other putative risks often attached to this drug—the potential for addiction, for instance, or for marijuana serving as a "gateway" to further drug abuse—were much overstated. The report urged further study to determine the real level of risk.

In examining the potential medical benefits of medical marijuana, the IOM report was equally cautious. It described relief from nausea associated with cancer chemotherapy, appetite stimulation for cancer and HIV patients, and treatment of muscle spasticity for patients with multiple sclerosis or spinal cord injury. Though these benefits seem real, the authors of the IOM report point out that we really don't know yet if they are significant or valuable enough to warrant the use of medical marijuana. Again, the report urged further study to determine the real level of benefit.

The Government Is Blocking Research

However, in the seven years since the IOM report was issued, virtually no research on potential risks and benefits has been done, because the government has blocked such studies. So,

FDA vs. Researchers

The Food and Drug Administration [FDA] issued a statement in April [2006] that no sound scientific studies support the medicinal use of marijuana for treatment. This conclusion left some researchers puzzled.

"I don't understand where that came from," said John Benson, M.D., ... who chaired an Institute of Medicine panel that wrote a ... report, "Marijuana and Medicine," ... published in 1999. "We found sufficient evidence that [smoking marijuana] had benefits for some patients, such as to help with nausea and chemotherapy for cancer treatment."

Renee Twombly,
"Despite Research, FDA Says Marijuana Has No Benefit,"
Journal of the National Cancer Institute, *July 5, 2006.*

we know neither more nor less [in 2006] about medical marijuana than we did seven years ago, whatever the FDA says. Why would the agency inaccurately claim that the science is settled when it isn't? I hardly need to say it: This isn't a medical or scientific conclusion. It's a political one.

This is certainly not the first time that politics has trumped science at the FDA. Another recent example: the agency's decision to block over-the-counter availability for emergency contraceptives in the face of overwhelming evidence that the treatment is safe and effective, and support for over-the-counter availability by the FDA's own advisory committee. From my standpoint as a doctor, the question is this: What do you do when federal agencies become so politicized that their recommendations can't necessarily be trusted? Do you have to treat other things they say as suspect? I depend on good advice and honest information from government agencies in the daily conduct of my work. I need to know what epidemic illnesses are circulating in my neighborhood even if that information might put a government agency in a bad light. I need to be able to trust government-sponsored research (especially because, goodness knows, I have learned not to trust manufacturer-sponsored research). I need to know that the advice I glean from government-sponsored agency websites will lead to the best care for my patients.

Marijuana as a medicine—whatever its risks and benefits are eventually determined to be—may turn out to be much less important than the question of whether we can count on agencies like the FDA to be honest in their dealings.

| "By mocking the idea of lawful behavior, legalization of medical marijuana may be more socially destructive than full legalization."

State Medical Marijuana Laws Undermine the Rule of Federal Law

George F. Will

George F. Will is a newspaper columnist, a journalist, and an author. In the following viewpoint, he argues that medical marijuana legislation in Colorado and California is being used as an excuse to sell pot for recreational use. He says that the federal government's decision not to prosecute medical marijuana users in states where medical marijuana is legal has contributed to rampant abuse of the system. He questions the benefits of legalization and argues that medical marijuana laws undermine the rule of law.

As you read, consider the following questions:

1. Who is John Suthers, according to Will?

2. According to Will, what percentage of Californians support legalization?

3. Why do Colorado's medical marijuana dispensaries want to be taxed and regulated, according to Will?

Inside the green neon sign, which is shaped like a marijuana leaf, is a red cross. The cross serves the fiction that most transactions in the store—which is what it really is—involve medicine.

Customers, Not Patients

The Justice Department recently [2009] announced that federal laws against marijuana would not be enforced for possession of marijuana that conforms to states' laws. In 2000, Colorado legalized medical marijuana. Since Justice's decision, the average age of the 400 persons a day seeking "prescriptions" at Colorado's multiplying medical marijuana dispensaries has fallen precipitously. Many new customers are college students.

Customers—this, not patients, is what most really are—tell doctors at the dispensaries that they suffer from insomnia, anxiety, headaches, premenstrual syndrome, "chronic pain," whatever, and pay nominal fees for "prescriptions." Most really just want to smoke pot.

So says Colorado's attorney general, John Suthers, an honest and thoughtful man trying to save his state from institutionalizing such hypocrisy. His dilemma is becoming commonplace: Thirteen states have, and fifteen more are considering, laws permitting medical use of marijuana.

Realizing they could not pass legalization of marijuana, some people who favor that campaigned to amend Colorado's Constitution to legalize sales for medicinal purposes. Marijuana has medical uses—e.g., to control nausea caused by chemotherapy—but the helpful ingredients can be conveyed with other medicines. Medical marijuana was legalized but, Suthers

HAU101-TS

"What'd I tell ya, ain't that good sh**? ... I mean ... yes, that prescription should help your eyesight."

"What'd I tell ya, ain't that good sh**?," cartoon by Toos, Andrew. www.CartoonStock .com. Copyright © Toos, Andrew. Reproduction rights obtainable from www.Cartoon Stock.com.

says, no serious regime was then developed to regulate who could buy—or grow—it. (Caregivers? For how many patients? And in what quantities, and for what "medical uses"?)

Today, Colorado communities can use zoning to restrict dispensaries or can ban them because, even if federal policy regarding medical marijuana is passivity, selling marijuana remains against federal law. But Colorado's probable future has unfolded in California, which in 1996 legalized sales of marijuana to persons with doctors' "prescriptions."

Legalization Through Medical Marijuana

Fifty-six percent of Californians support legalization, and Roger Parloff reports [in *Fortune* magazine] that they essentially have this. He notes that many California "patients" arrive at dispensaries "on bicycles, roller skates or skateboards." A

Los Angeles city councilman estimates that there are about 600 dispensaries in the city. If so, they outnumber the Starbucks stores there.

The councilman wants to close dispensaries whose intent is profit rather than "compassionate" distribution of medicine. Good luck with that: Privacy considerations will shield doctors from investigations of their lucrative 15-minute transactions with "patients."

Colorado's medical marijuana dispensaries have hired lobbyists to seek taxation and regulation, for the same reason Nevada's brothel industry wants to be taxed and regulated by the state: The Nevada Brothel [Owners] Association regards taxation as legitimation and insurance against prohibition as the booming state's frontier mentality recedes.

State governments, misunderstanding markets and ravenous for revenue, exaggerate the potential windfall from taxing legalized marijuana. California thinks it might reap $1.4 billion. But Rosalie [Liccardo] Pacula, a RAND Corp. economist, estimates that prohibition raises marijuana production costs at least 400 percent, so legalization would cause prices to fall much more than the 50 percent assumed by the $1.4 billion estimate.

Furthermore, marijuana is a normal good in that demand for it varies with price. Legalization, by drastically lowering price, will increase marijuana's public health costs, including mental and respiratory problems, and motor vehicle accidents.

States attempting to use high taxes to keep marijuana prices artificially high would leave a large market for much cheaper illegal—unregulated and untaxed—marijuana. So revenue (and law enforcement savings) would depend on the price falling close to the cost of production. In the 1990s, a mere $2 per pack difference between U.S. and Canadian cigarette prices created such a smuggling problem that Canada repealed a cigarette tax increase.

Suthers has multiple drug-related worries. Colorado ranks sixth in the nation in identity theft, two-thirds of which is driven by the state's $1.4 billion annual methamphetamine addiction. He is loath to see complete legalization of marijuana at a moment when new methods of cultivation are producing plants in which the active ingredient, THC [tetrahydrocannabinol], is "seven, eight times as concentrated" as it used to be. Furthermore, he was pleasantly surprised when a survey of nonusing young people revealed that health concerns did not explain nonuse. The main explanation was the law: "We underestimate the number of people who care that something is illegal."

But they will care less as law itself loses its dignity. By mocking the idea of lawful behavior, legalization of medical marijuana may be more socially destructive than full legalization.

> *"They're protecting the argument that medical marijuana is out of control by interfering with efforts to control it. It's a slippery and typical drug war propaganda tactic."*

The Federal Government's Attacks on Medical Marijuana Result in Abuse and Injustice

Scott Morgan

Scott Morgan is associate editor of StoptheDrugWar.org. In the following viewpoint, he argues that the Barack Obama administration has gone back on its promises not to target medical marijuana users who are in compliance with state law. Morgan says that the federal government is trying to interfere with states' legalization of medical marijuana. He argues that the campaign is senseless and an overreach of federal authority. He says that medical marijuana has many benefits and that states must push back against federal interference.

As you read, consider the following questions:

1. What states have received federal cautions about medical marijuana, according to the viewpoint?

2. What evidence does Morgan present to suggest that the threat of prosecuting state employees or state-licensed businesses is simply a scare tactic?

3. What benefits does Morgan list as arising from the medical marijuana industry?

When Attorney General Eric Holder announced in October 2009 that the Dept. of Justice [DOJ] would respect state medical marijuana laws, the nation breathed a collective sigh of relief. By that time, any lingering support for aggressive federal raids on medical marijuana providers had dwindled into invisibility. The American people wanted to see patients protected, and [President Barack] Obama's pledge to do so earned him nothing but praise from both the press and the public.

Targeting Medical Marijuana

Unfortunately, recent months have brought about what can only be described as the rapid collapse of the Obama administration's support for medical marijuana. Following dozens of aggressive DEA [Drug Enforcement Administration] raids, along with some unusual IRS [Internal Revenue Service] audits, the Dept. of Justice has now begun openly endeavoring to destroy carefully regulated state programs before they get off the ground:

> Olympia, Wash.—Several states have started reassessing their medical marijuana laws after stern warnings from the federal government that everyone from licensed growers to regulators could be subjected to prosecution.
>
> The ominous-sounding letters from U.S. attorneys in recent weeks [in 2011] have directly injected the federal govern-

ment back into a debate that has for years been progressing at the state level. Warnings in Washington State led Gov. Chris Gregoire to veto a proposal that would have created licensed marijuana dispensaries.

Letters with various cautions have also gone to officials in California, Colorado, Montana and Rhode Island.

It's a sweeping intervention that instantly divorces the Obama administration from its stated policy of not focusing resources on individuals who are clearly compliant with state law. Unlike the numerous recent dispensary raids, which could theoretically result from competing interpretations of state law, this new incursion constitutes a direct threat of arrest against state employees acting in good faith to administer perfectly lawful state programs.

The mindlessness of all this operates on multiple levels, beginning with the fact that no state employee or state-licensed business has ever actually been prosecuted for involvement with medical marijuana. The suggestion that they'd do such a thing is nothing more than a cynical scare tactic aimed at stalling the numerous state programs moving forward this year.

The notion that DOJ would indict state regulators shouldn't even be entertained, let alone held up as a prohibitive obstacle to implementing tightly controlled programs. Think about how ridiculous that is. Would they prosecute Health Dept. staffers in Rhode Island, which only allows three nonprofit dispensaries, even though DOJ took no action against officials in states like Colorado and California with fewer restrictions and far more marijuana businesses? The damage to DOJ's credibility would be so extraordinary, one almost wishes they were foolish enough to try it.

Medical Marijuana Must Move Forward

The federal agenda is obviously to avoid allowing state regulation to further legitimize the industry, and they're willing to

Large Majority Favors Allowing Medical Marijuana in Their State

Your state allowing the sale and use of marijuana for medical purposes...	March 2010 %
Favor	73
Oppose	23
Don't know	4

Should the use of marijuana be made legal?	2008	2010
Yes	35	41
No	57	52
Don't know	8	7

TAKEN FROM: Pew Research Center for the People & the Press, "Public Support for Legalizing Medical Marijuana," April 1, 2010. www.people-press.org.

keep things messier than necessary just so they can continue citing that messiness as evidence that this can't work. They're protecting the argument that medical marijuana is out of control by interfering with efforts to control it. It's a slippery and typical drug war propaganda tactic that, once understood and exposed, should begin to lose its potency.

For 15 years now, opponents of medical marijuana have been saying this can't be done because it's illegal under federal law. Yet today [in 2011], medical marijuana is a $1.7 billion industry that is helping sick people, creating jobs, generating substantial tax revenue, and even taking money away from murderous cartels in Mexico. There is no reason, old or new, legal or practical, that this important progress can't continue.

The forward momentum of the marijuana reform movement now depends on the willingness of state officials to take a stand against federal interference and reveal these empty threats for what they are. But beyond that, the time has come for the American public to send a message to the president who promised more compassionate policies than his predecessor. If Obama hasn't yet figured out how the American public feels about the war on medical marijuana, then let us each take a moment to politely remind him.

Periodical and Internet Sources Bibliography

The following articles have been selected to supplement the diverse views presented in this chapter.

Paul Armentano	"What's Behind the Obama Administration's About Face Regarding Medical Marijuana?," *Huffington Post*, May 5, 2011. www.huffington post.com.
Mike Baker	"WA Medical Marijuana Dispensaries Left Vulnerable," *Seattle Times*, May 24, 2011.
Katie Boer	"Rampant Medical Marijuana Abuse Attracting Drug Trafficking to Southern Oregon," KPIC, March 15, 2010. www.kpic.com.
Erica Bolstad	"Alaska Policy on Medical Marijuana Remains Intact," *Anchorage Daily News*, October 25, 2009.
Mick Dumke	"House Republican Leader Tom Cross Explains Why He Supports a New Medical Marijuana Bill," *Chicago Reader*, May 3, 2011.
Huffington Post	"Illinois Medical Marijuana Bill Fails Again, Despite Republican Support," May 5, 2011. www.huffingtonpost.com.
Jennifer McKee	"State Lawmakers Say Medical Marijuana Abuse Is 'Out of Control,'" *Helena Independent Record*, July 14, 2010.
NORML	"Alaska Marijuana Penalties," November 5, 2010. www.natlnorml.org.
David Schwartz	"Arizona to Sue to Clarify Medical Marijuana Act," Reuters, May 24, 2011. www.reuters.com.
William Yardley	"New Federal Crackdown Confounds States That Allow Medical Marijuana," *New York Times*, May 7, 2011.

Chapter 4

Should Recreational Marijuana Be Legalized?

Chapter Preface

Some religions include use of marijuana as a sacrament or as part of their rituals. Among the best known of these is Rastafarianism. Rastafarianism is a mystical religion based in Christianity that gained popularity among descendents of slaves in Jamaica. Marijuana, or ganja, is seen by Rastafarians as a way to get in touch with nature and also as a way to distinguish themselves and their community from non-Rastafarians. According to Mark LeVine in an article on Beliefnet,

> Scholars and Rastas alike consider marijuana use among the most dominant force in the movement's religious ideology and their strongest shared experience. Rastas say its use is prescribed by biblical verses such as Psalm 104:14, where it is written "He causeth the grass for the cattle, and herb for the service of man." . . . The controlled ritual smoking of "wisdomweed" is advocated as "an incense pleasing to the Lord"; it is a core activity in their daily life, both a "sacrament" and an aid to meditation.

The religious use of ganja has raised legal issues in the United States. Rastafarians have said that their use of ganja should be protected under the First Amendment, which guarantees freedom of religion. Some Native American tribes have used similar arguments and have been permitted by the government to use the hallucinogen peyote in their religious ceremonies. "By contrast, Rastafarians have been less successful in persuading the courts to view their belief system as a religion, while the fact that they use marijuana on a regular basis—not for identifiable ceremonies—probably contributes to a perception of this as cultural rather than religious," according to Anne Phillips in *Multiculturalism Without Culture*.

US courts have also been reluctant to use First Amendment exemptions to allow Rastafarians to import marijuana.

For example, a January 6, 2003, article in *Cannabis Culture* magazine detailed a case in which Ras Iyah Ben Makahna of the US territory of Guam was cleared of possession charges because of his Rastafarian faith, but his smuggling convictions were upheld by the Ninth Circuit Court. "Rastafarianism does not require importation of a controlled substance, which increases availability of a controlled substance and makes it harder for Guam to control," the judge stated.

This chapter looks at other debates surrounding the legalization of marijuana for non-medical uses.

> "Enforcing marijuana prohibition costs taxpayers an estimated $10 billion annually and results in the arrest of more than 829,000 individuals per year."

Responsible Adult Personal Use of Marijuana Should Be Legalized

NORML

NORML (National Organization for the Reform of Marijuana Laws) is a nonprofit lobbying organization working to legalize marijuana. In the following viewpoint, NORML argues that marijuana use should be decriminalized and eventually legalized for responsible adult use. NORML says that marijuana is safer than alcohol and tobacco and that the effort to criminalize it has resulted in a huge expenditure and in the arrest of many otherwise law-abiding citizens. NORML also notes that in areas where decriminalization has been enacted, there has been little increase in marijuana use.

As you read, consider the following questions:

1. In what way did Massachusetts decriminalize marijuana, according to NORML?

2. According to government surveys, how many people use marijuana?

3. What activities besides marijuana use does NORML suggest are inappropriate for children?

NORML [National Organization for the Reform of Marijuana Laws] supports the removal of all penalties for the private possession and responsible use of marijuana by adults, including cultivation for personal use, and casual nonprofit transfers of small amounts. This policy, known as decriminalization, removes the consumer—the marijuana smoker—from the criminal justice system, while maintaining criminal penalties against those who sell or traffic large quantities of the drug.

Experts Recommend Decriminalization

In 1972, President Richard Nixon's National Commission on Marihuana and Drug Abuse recommended that Congress adopt this policy nationally in the United States. Since then, more than a dozen government-appointed commissions in both the U.S. and abroad have recommended similar actions. None of these commissions have endorsed continuing to arrest and jail minor marijuana offenders. . . .

Since 1973, 13 state legislatures [as of March 2009]— Alaska, California, Colorado, Maine, [Michigan,] Minnesota, Mississippi, Nebraska, Nevada, New York, North Carolina, Ohio and Oregon—have enacted versions of marijuana decriminalization. In November 2008, Massachusetts voters passed a statewide initiative making the possession of up to one ounce of marijuana an infraction punishable by no more than a $100 fine. The law took effect on January 2, 2009. In each of these states, marijuana users no longer face jail time (nor in most cases, arrest or criminal records) for the possession or use of small amounts of marijuana. According to national polls, voters overwhelmingly support these policies. In

Oregon, voters recently reaffirmed their state's decriminalization law by a 2-1 margin in a statewide referendum.

More than 30 percent of the U.S. population lives under some form of marijuana decriminalization, and according to government and academic studies, these laws have not contributed to an increase in marijuana consumption nor negatively impacted adolescent attitudes toward drug use. . . .

Enforcing marijuana prohibition costs taxpayers an estimated $10 billion annually and results in the arrest of more than 829,000 individuals per year—far more than the total number of arrestees for all violent crimes combined, including murder, rape, robbery and aggravated assault. This policy is a tremendous waste of national and state criminal justice resources that should be focused on combating serious and violent crime. In addition, it invites government unnecessarily into areas of our private lives, and needlessly damages the lives and careers of hundreds of thousands of otherwise law-abiding citizens. NORML believes now, as former president Jimmy Carter told Congress in 1977, that: "Penalties against drug use should not be more damaging to an individual than the use of the drug itself. Nowhere is this more clear than in the laws against the possession of marijuana in private for personal use."

Responsible Use

Marijuana is the third most popular recreational drug in America (behind only alcohol and tobacco), and has been used by nearly 100 million Americans. According to government surveys, some 25 million Americans have smoked marijuana in the past year, and more than 14 million do so regularly despite harsh laws against its use. Our public policies should reflect this reality, not deny it.

Marijuana is far less dangerous than alcohol or tobacco. Around 50,000 people die each year from alcohol poisoning. Similarly, more than 400,000 deaths each year are attributed

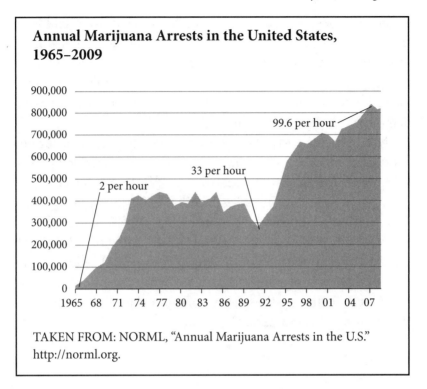

Annual Marijuana Arrests in the United States, 1965–2009

TAKEN FROM: NORML, "Annual Marijuana Arrests in the U.S." http://norml.org.

to tobacco smoking. By comparison, marijuana is nontoxic and cannot cause death by overdose. According to the prestigious European medical journal, the *Lancet*, "The smoking of cannabis, even long term, is not harmful to health. . . . It would be reasonable to judge cannabis as less of a threat . . . than alcohol or tobacco."

As with alcohol consumption, marijuana smoking can never be an excuse for misconduct or other improper behavior. For example, driving or operating heavy equipment while impaired from marijuana should be prohibited.

Most importantly, marijuana smoking is for adults only, and is inappropriate for children. There are many activities in our society that are permissible for adults, but forbidden for children, such as motorcycle riding, skydiving, signing contracts, getting married, drinking alcohol or smoking tobacco. However, we do not condone arresting adults who responsibly engage in these activities in order to dissuade our children from doing so. Nor can we justify arresting adult marijuana smokers on the grounds of sending a "message" to children. Our expectation and hope for young people is that they grow up to be responsible adults, and our obligation to them is to demonstrate what that means. . . .

NORML supports the eventual development of a legally controlled market for marijuana, where consumers could buy marijuana for personal use from a safe legal source. This policy, generally known as legalization, exists on various levels in a handful of European countries like the Netherlands and Switzerland, both of which enjoy lower rates of adolescent marijuana use than the U.S. Such a system would reduce many of the problems presently associated with the prohibition of marijuana, including the crime, corruption and violence associated with a "black market."

| "*Marijuana is a dangerous substance that should remain illegal under state law.*"

Marijuana Should Not Be Legalized

Charles Stimson

Charles "Cully" Stimson is a senior legal fellow in the Center for Legal and Judicial Studies at the Heritage Foundation. In the following viewpoint, he argues that the California ballot initiative to decriminalize marijuana is dangerous and impractical. He argues that marijuana is more addictive and more dangerous than alcohol and that legalizing it is unsafe. He also says that legalizing marijuana on the state level despite federal prohibitions will result in difficulties for localities. He adds that the ballot measure is unconstitutional.

As you read, consider the following questions:

1. What does Stimson say are the health benefits of alcohol consumption?

2. What evidence does Stimson provide that a high number of criminals are marijuana users?

Charles Stimson, "Legalizing Marijuana: Why Citizens Should Just Say No," Heritage Foundation, Legal Memorandum, no. 56, September 13, 2010. www.heritage.org. Copyright © 2010 by The Heritage Foundation. All rights reserved. Reproduced by permission.

3. What effect does the RAND Corporation think legalization will have on the price of marijuana, and what other negative effects would that have?

The scientific literature is clear that marijuana is addictive and that its use significantly impairs bodily and mental functions. Marijuana use is associated with memory loss, cancer, immune system deficiencies, heart disease, and birth defects, among other conditions. Even where decriminalized, marijuana trafficking remains a source of violence, crime, and social disintegration.

The California Ballot Initiative

Nonetheless, this November [2010], California voters will consider a ballot initiative, the Regulate, Control and Tax Cannabis Act of 2010 (RCTCA), that would legalize most marijuana distribution and use under state law. (These activities would remain federal crimes.) This vote is the culmination of an organized campaign by pro-marijuana activists stretching back decades.

The current campaign, like previous efforts, downplays the well-documented harms of marijuana trafficking and use while promising benefits ranging from reduced crime to additional tax revenue. In particular, supporters of the initiative make five bold claims:

1. "Marijuana is safe and nonaddictive."

2. "Marijuana prohibition makes no more sense than alcohol prohibition did in the early 1900s."

3. "The government's efforts to combat illegal drugs have been a total failure."

4. "The money spent on government efforts to combat the illegal drug trade can be better spent on substance abuse and treatment for the allegedly few marijuana users who abuse the drug."

5. "Tax revenue collected from marijuana sales would substantially outweigh the social costs of legalization."

As this [viewpoint] details, all five claims are demonstrably false or, based on the best evidence, highly dubious.

Further, supporters of the initiative simply ignore the mechanics of decriminalization—that is, how it would directly affect law enforcement, crime, and communities. Among the important questions left unanswered are:

- How would the state law fit into a federal regime that prohibits marijuana production, distribution, and possession?

- Would decriminalization, especially if combined with taxation, expand market opportunities for the gangs and cartels that currently dominate drug distribution?

- Would existing zoning laws prohibit marijuana cultivation in residential neighborhoods, and if not, what measures would growers have to undertake to keep children from the plants?

- Would transportation providers be prohibited from firing bus drivers because they smoke marijuana?

No one knows the specifics of how marijuana decriminalization would work in practice or what measures would be necessary to prevent children, teenagers, criminals, and addicts from obtaining the drug.

The federal government shares these concerns. Gil Kerlikowske, director of the White House Office of National Drug Control Policy (ONDCP), recently stated, "Marijuana legalization, for any purpose, is a non-starter in the [Barack] Obama administration." The administration—widely viewed as more liberal than any other in recent memory and, for a time, as embodying the hopes of pro-legalization activists—has weighed the costs and benefits and concluded that marijuana legalization would compromise public health and safety.

California's voters, if they take a fair-minded look at the evidence and the practical problems of legalization, should reach the same conclusion: Marijuana is a dangerous substance that should remain illegal under state law.

Marijuana Is Less Safe than Alcohol

The RCTCA's purpose, as defined by advocates of legalization, is to regulate marijuana just as the government regulates alcohol. The law would allow anyone 21 years of age or older to possess, process, share, or transport up to one full ounce of marijuana "for personal consumption." Individuals could possess an unlimited number of living and harvested marijuana plants on the premises where they were grown. Individual landowners or lawful occupants of private property could cultivate marijuana plants "for personal consumption" in an area of not more than 25 square feet per private residence or parcel.

The RCTCA would legalize drug-related paraphernalia and tools and would license establishments for on-site smoking and other consumption of marijuana. Supporters have included some alcohol-like restrictions against, for example, smoking marijuana while operating a vehicle. Finally, the act authorizes the imposition and collection of taxes and fees associated with legalization of marijuana.

Marijuana advocates have had some success peddling the notion that marijuana is a "soft" drug, similar to alcohol, and fundamentally different from "hard" drugs like cocaine or heroin. It is true that marijuana is not the most dangerous of the commonly abused drugs, but that is not to say that it is safe. Indeed, marijuana shares more in common with the "hard" drugs than it does with alcohol.

A common argument for legalization is that smoking marijuana is no more dangerous than drinking alcohol and that prohibiting the use of marijuana is therefore no more justified than the prohibition of alcohol. As Jacob Sullum, author of *Saying Yes: In Defense of Drug Use*, writes:

> Americans understood the problems associated with alcohol abuse, but they also understood the problems associated with Prohibition, which included violence, organized crime, official corruption, the erosion of civil liberties, disrespect for the law, and injuries and deaths caused by tainted black-market booze. They decided that these unintended side effects far outweighed whatever harms Prohibition prevented by discouraging drinking. The same sort of analysis today would show that the harm caused by drug prohibition far outweighs the harm it prevents, even without taking into account the value to each individual of being sovereign over his own body and mind.

At first blush, this argument is appealing, especially to those wary of overregulation by government. But it overlooks the enormous difference between alcohol and marijuana.

Legalization advocates claim that marijuana and alcohol are mild intoxicants and so should be regulated similarly; but as the experience of nearly every culture, over the thousands of years of human history demonstrates, alcohol is different. Nearly every culture has its own alcoholic preparations, and nearly all have successfully regulated alcohol consumption through cultural norms. The same cannot be said of marijuana. There are several possible explanations for alcohol's unique status: For most people, it is not addictive; it is rarely consumed to the point of intoxication; low-level consumption is consistent with most manual and intellectual tasks; it has several positive health benefits; and it is formed by the fermentation of many common substances and easily metabolized by the body.

To be sure, there are costs associated with alcohol abuse, such as drunk driving and disease associated with excessive consumption. A few cultures—and this nation for a short while during Prohibition—have concluded that the benefits of

153

alcohol consumption are not worth the costs. But they are the exception; most cultures have concluded that it is acceptable in moderation. No other intoxicant shares that status.

Alcohol differs from marijuana in several crucial respects. First, marijuana is far more likely to cause addiction. Second, it is usually consumed to the point of intoxication. Third, it has no known general healthful properties, though it may have some palliative effects. Fourth, it is toxic and deleterious to health. Thus, while it is true that both alcohol and marijuana are less intoxicating than other mood-altering drugs, that is not to say that marijuana is especially similar to alcohol or that its use is healthy or even safe.

In fact, compared to alcohol, marijuana is not safe. Long-term, moderate consumption of alcohol carries few health risks and even offers some significant benefits. For example, a glass of wine (or other alcoholic drink) with dinner actually improves health. Dozens of peer-reviewed medical studies suggest that drinking moderate amounts of alcohol reduces the risk of heart disease, strokes, gallstones, diabetes, and death from a heart attack. According to the Mayo Clinic, among many others, moderate use of alcohol (defined as two drinks a day) "seems to offer some health benefits, particularly for the heart." Countless articles in medical journals and other scientific literature confirm the positive health effects of moderate alcohol consumption.

Marijuana Has Negative Health Effects

The effects of regular marijuana consumption are quite different. For example, the National Institute on Drug Abuse (a division of the National Institutes of Health) has released studies showing that use of marijuana has wide-ranging negative health effects. Long-term marijuana consumption "impairs the ability of T-cells in the lungs' immune system to fight off some infections." These studies have also found that marijuana consumption impairs short-term memory, making it

Alcohol vs. Marijuana

[Charles] Cully Stimson: [There] is no doubt that alcohol is destructive when used to excess, period. . . . [But] we're not talking about the people at the margins who abuse it. We're talking about . . . if it's used the way it's intended, not to excess. So if you compare alcohol next to marijuana, . . . alcohol has arguably good things that it does for you and marijuana—nobody, no credible research has come out to say smoking marijuana is good for you. Yes, I'm sure it makes you feel better. I'm sure of it.

"Transcript: Thom Hartmann Asks 'Cully' Stimson, Should We Legalize Pot or Criminalize Alcohol?," Thom Hartmann Program, October 14, 2010. www.thomhartmann.com.

difficult to learn and retain information or perform complex tasks; slows reaction time and impairs motor coordination; increases heart rate by 20 percent to 100 percent, thus elevating the risk of heart attack; and alters moods, resulting in artificial euphoria, calmness, or (in high doses) anxiety or paranoia. And it gets worse: Marijuana has toxic properties that can result in birth defects, pain, respiratory system damage, brain damage, and stroke.

Further, prolonged use of marijuana may cause cognitive degradation and is "associated with lower test scores and lower educational attainment because during periods of intoxication the drug affects the ability to learn and process information, thus influencing attention, concentration, and short-term memory." Unlike alcohol, marijuana has been shown to have a residual effect on cognitive ability that persists beyond the period of intoxication. According to the National Institute on Drug Abuse, whereas alcohol is broken down relatively quickly in the human body, THC (tetrahydrocannabinol, the main active chemical in marijuana) is stored in organs and fatty tissues, allowing it to remain in a user's body for days or even weeks after consumption. Research has shown that marijuana consumption may also cause "psychotic symptoms."

Marijuana's effects on the body are profound. According to the British Lung Foundation, "smoking three or four marijuana joints is as bad for your lungs as smoking twenty tobacco cigarettes." Researchers in Canada found that marijuana smoke contains significantly higher levels of numerous toxic compounds, like ammonia and hydrogen cyanide, than regular tobacco smoke. In fact, the study determined that ammonia was found in marijuana smoke at levels of up to 20 times the levels found in tobacco. Similarly, hydrogen cyanide was found in marijuana smoke at concentrations three to five times greater than those found in tobacco smoke.

Marijuana, like tobacco, is addictive. One study found that more than 30 percent of adults who used marijuana in the course of a year were dependent on the drug. These individuals often show signs of withdrawal and compulsive behavior. Marijuana dependence is also responsible for a large proportion of calls to drug abuse help lines and treatment centers.

To equate marijuana use with alcohol consumption is, at best, uninformed and, at worst, actively misleading. Only in the most superficial ways are the two substances alike, and they differ in every way that counts: addictiveness, toxicity, health effects, and risk of intoxication.

Unintended Consequences

Today, marijuana trafficking is linked to a variety of crimes, from assault and murder to money laundering and smuggling. Legalization of marijuana would increase demand for the drug and almost certainly exacerbate drug-related crime, as well as cause a myriad of unintended but predictable consequences.

To begin with, an astonishingly high percentage of criminals are marijuana users. According to a study by the RAND Corporation, approximately 60 percent of arrestees test positive for marijuana use in the United States, England, and Australia. Further, marijuana metabolites are found in arrestees' urine more frequently than those of any other drug.

Although some studies have shown marijuana to inhibit aggressive behavior and violence, the National Research Council concluded that the "long-term use of marijuana may alter the nervous system in ways that do promote violence." No place serves as a better example than Amsterdam.

Marijuana advocates often point to the Netherlands as a well-functioning society with a relaxed attitude toward drugs, but they rarely mention that Amsterdam is one of Europe's most violent cities. In Amsterdam, officials are in the process of closing marijuana dispensaries, or "coffee shops," because of the crime associated with their operation. Furthermore, the Dutch Ministry of Health, Welfare and Sport has expressed "concern about drug and alcohol use among young people and the social consequences, which range from poor school performance and truancy to serious impairment, including brain damage."

Amsterdam's experience is already being duplicated in California under the current medical marijuana statute. In Los Angeles, police report that areas surrounding cannabis clubs have experienced a 200 percent increase in robberies, a 52.2 percent increase in burglaries, a 57.1 percent increase in aggravated assault, and a 130.8 percent increase in burglaries from automobiles. Current law requires a doctor's prescription to procure marijuana; full legalization would likely spark an even more acute increase in crime.

Legalization of marijuana would also inflict a series of negative consequences on neighborhoods and communities. The nuisance caused by the powerful odor of mature marijuana plants is already striking California municipalities. The

City Council of Chico, California, has released a report detailing the situation and describing how citizens living near marijuana cultivators are disturbed by the incredible stink emanating from the plants.

Perhaps worse than the smell, crime near growers is increasing, associated with "the theft of marijuana from yards where it is being grown." As a result, housing prices near growers are sinking.

The Details of Implementation

Theoretical arguments in favor of marijuana legalization usually overlook the practical matter of how the drug would be regulated and sold. It is the details of implementation, of course, that will determine the effect of legalization on families, schools, and communities. Most basically, how and where would marijuana be sold?

- Would neighborhoods become neon red-light districts like Amsterdam's, accompanied by the same crime and social disorder?

- If so, who decides what neighborhoods will be so afflicted—residents and landowners or far-off government officials?

- Or would marijuana sales be so widespread that users could add it to their grocery lists?

- If so, how would stores sell it, how would they store it, and how would they prevent it from being diverted into the gray market?

- Would stores dealing in marijuana have to fortify their facilities to reduce the risk of theft and assault?

The most likely result is that the drug will not be sold in legitimate stores at all, because while the federal government is currently tolerating medical marijuana dispensaries, it will not tolerate wide-scale sales under general legalizational statutes. So marijuana will continue to be sold on the gray or black market.

The act does not answer these or other practical questions regarding implementation. Rather, it leaves those issues to localities. No doubt, those entities will pass a variety of laws in an attempt to deal with the many problems caused by legalization, unless the local laws are struck down by California courts as inconsistent with the underlying initiative, which would be even worse. At best, that patchwork of laws, differing from one locality to another, will be yet another unintended and predictable problem arising from legalization as envisioned under this act.

Citizens also should not overlook what may be the greatest harms of marijuana legalization: increased addiction to and use of harder drugs. In addition to marijuana's harmful effects on the body and relationship to criminal conduct, it is a gateway drug that can lead users to more dangerous drugs. Prosecutors, judges, police officers, detectives, parole or probation officers, and even defense attorneys know that the vast majority of defendants arrested for violent crimes test positive for illegal drugs, including marijuana. They also know that marijuana is the starter drug of choice for most criminals. Whereas millions of Americans consume moderate amounts of alcohol without ever "moving on" to dangerous drugs, marijuana use and cocaine use are strongly correlated.

While correlation does not necessarily reflect causation, and while the science is admittedly mixed as to whether it is the drug itself or the people the new user associates with who cause the move on to cocaine, heroin, LSD, or other drugs, the RAND Corporation reports that marijuana prices and cocaine use are directly linked, suggesting a substitution effect between the two drugs. Moreover, according to RAND, legalization will cause marijuana prices to fall as much as 80 percent. That can lead to significant consequences because "a 10-percent decrease in the price of marijuana would increase the prevalence of cocaine use by 4.4 to 4.9 percent." As cheap marijuana floods the market both in and outside of California, use of many different types of drugs will increase, as will marijuana use.

It is impossible to predict the precise consequences of legalization, but the experiences of places that have eased restrictions on marijuana are not positive. Already, California is suffering crime, dislocation, and increased drug use under its current regulatory scheme. Further liberalizing the law will only make matters worse.

Flouting Federal Law

Another area of great uncertainty is how a state law legalizing marijuana would fit in with federal law to the contrary. Congress has enacted a comprehensive regulatory scheme for restricting access to illicit drugs and other controlled substances. The Controlled Substances Act of 1970 prohibits the manufacture, distribution, and possession of all substances deemed to be schedule I drugs—drugs like heroin, PCP, and cocaine. Because marijuana has no "currently accepted medical use in treatment in the United States," it is a schedule I drug that cannot be bought, sold, possessed, or used without violating federal law.

Under the Supremacy Clause of the Constitution of the United States, the Controlled Substances Act is the supreme law of the land and cannot be superseded by state laws that purport to contradict or abrogate its terms. The RCTCA proposes to "reform California's cannabis laws in a way that will benefit our state" and "[r]egulate cannabis like we do alcohol." But the act does not even purport to address the fundamental constitutional infirmity that it would be in direct conflict with federal law. If enacted and unchallenged by the federal government, it would call into question the government's ability to regulate all controlled substances, including drugs such as

Oxycontin, methamphetamine, heroin, and powder and crack cocaine. More likely, however, the feds would challenge the law in court, and the courts would have no choice but to strike it down. . . .

If the RCTCA were enacted, it would conflict with the provisions of the Controlled Substances Act and invite extensive litigation that would almost certainly result in its being struck down. Until that happened, state law enforcement officers would be forced into a position of uncertainty regarding their conflicting obligations under federal and state law and cooperation with federal authorities.

Bogus Economics

An innovation of the campaign in support of RCTCA is its touting of the potential benefit of legalization to the government, in terms of additional revenues from taxing marijuana and savings from backing down in the "war on drugs." The National Organization for the Reform of Marijuana Laws (NORML), for example, claims that legalization "could yield California taxpayers over $1.2 billion per year" in tax benefits. According to a California NORML report updated in October 2009, an excise tax of $50 per ounce would raise about $770 million to $900 million per year and save over $200 million in law enforcement costs per year. It is worth noting that $900 million equates to 18 million ounces—enough marijuana for Californians to smoke one billion marijuana cigarettes each year.

But these projections are highly speculative and riddled with unfounded assumptions. Dr. Rosalie Liccardo Pacula, an expert with the RAND Corporation who has studied the economics of drug policy for over 15 years, has explained that the California "Board of Equalization's estimate of $1.4 billion [in] potential revenue for the state is based on a series of assumptions that are in some instances subject to tremendous uncertainty and in other cases not validated." She urged the

California Committee on Public Safety to conduct an honest and thorough cost-benefit analysis of the potential revenues and costs associated with legalizing marijuana. To date, no such realistic cost-benefit analysis has been done.

| "The budgetary impacts of marijuana legalization are not trivial. A savings of $7.7 billion per year in resources is substantial."

Legalizing Marijuana Would Save Money and Generate Tax Revenue

Jeffrey Miron

Jeffrey Miron is a professor of economics at Harvard University. In the following viewpoint, he argues that legalizing marijuana would provide the government with substantial economic benefits, first through ending costs associated with enforcement and second through revenue gained from taxing legal marijuana. He says that these economic benefits would be significant but not overwhelming. He adds, however, that there are many noneconomic costs associated with marijuana prohibition and few real benefits. As a result, he argues that marijuana prohibition should end.

Jeffrey Miron, "A Cost-Benefit Analysis of Legalizing Marijuana," *The Pot Book: A Complete Guide to Cannabis: Its Role in Medicine, Politics, Science, and Culture*, edited by Julie Holland. Rochester, VT: Park Street Press, 2010, pp. 447–453. Copyright © 2010 by Inner Traditions. All rights reserved. Reproduced by permission. www.InnerTraditions .com.

As you read, consider the following questions:

1. Why does Miron say that it is critical that marijuana is not taxed too excessively?

2. What does Miron say about the savings from marijuana legalization compared to the size of the US economy?

3. What does Miron believe should be done about the possibility of traffic accidents caused by marijuana smokers driving under the influence?

Government prohibition of marijuana is the subject of enormous debate. Advocates believe prohibition reduces marijuana trafficking and use, thereby discouraging crime, improving productivity, and increasing health. Critics believe prohibition has only modest effects on trafficking and use while causing many problems typically attributed to marijuana itself. In particular, prohibition does not eliminate the marijuana market but merely drives it underground, which has numerous unwanted consequences.

Marijuana and Government Budgets

One issue in this debate is the effect of marijuana prohibition on government budgets. Prohibition entails direct enforcement costs. If marijuana were legal, enforcement costs would be zero, and governments could levy taxes on the production and sale of marijuana. Thus, government expenditure would decline and tax revenue would increase. The reduction in expenditure constitutes a net saving in resources as well; that is, these funds would be available for other uses. The increase in tax revenues would be a transfer from drug users and producers to the general public. In attempting to change current policy, advocates of decriminalization or legalization have often emphasized these budgetary impacts as important pieces of their argument.

This [viewpoint] discusses issues related to the savings in government expenditure and the gains in tax revenue that would result from legalizing marijuana. The first section provides a brief review of existing estimates and discusses some limitations and caveats. The second section discusses the broad range of issues relevant to analyzing legalization versus prohibition and argues that legalization is the better policy even if the budgetary impacts are minor.

The Economic Effects of Marijuana Legalization

In a legalized marijuana regime, all criminal and civil penalties against production, distribution, sale, and possession would cease. Instead, marijuana would be treated like other legal goods subject to standard regulations and taxes. Policy might also impose marijuana-specific regulations and taxes, as occurs now for alcohol and tobacco. These should be moderate enough, however, that marijuana would be produced and distributed in a legal market, not driven underground.

This policy change would affect government budgets in the following ways. First, government would save the resources currently devoted to arresting, prosecuting, and incarcerating marijuana producers and consumers. Second, governments would collect tax revenue on the production and sale of legal marijuana. The tax rates on marijuana might be the same as those applied generally, or they might be higher, as with alcohol and tobacco.

Earlier research (Miron 2006) indicates that marijuana legalization would reduce government expenditures by roughly $8 billion annually. As shown in [the sidebar for this viewpoint], approximately $5.5 billion of this would come from decreased state and local expenditures and approximately $2.5 billion from decreased federal expenditures. At the state and local levels, the reduced expenditures would consist of $1.8 billion less spent on police, $3.2 less on prosecutions, and $0.5

billion less on incarceration. (At the federal level, a detailed breakdown is not readily available.)

Marijuana legalization would also generate tax revenue of approximately $2.4 billion annually if marijuana were taxed like all other goods, and $6.2 billion annually if marijuana were taxed at rates comparable to those on alcohol and tobacco. (A 2007 study from George Mason University reports that lost revenue from failing to tax a $113 billion business, as well as costs incurred enforcing marijuana laws, cost U.S. taxpayers $41.8 billion yearly.) These budgetary impacts rely on a range of assumptions, but the estimates are most likely biased downward. A few comments about these estimates are in order.

Taxes Should Be Moderate

The tax rates on legalized marijuana could be higher than those on most other goods. It is critical, however, that these rates not become so elevated that they drive the marijuana market underground and amount to de facto prohibition. Moreover, high tax rates have many of the same negatives as prohibition, such as penalizing marijuana users who consume responsibly. Thus assuming a legalized regime can generate huge revenues, or justifying legalization by asserting that high taxes will be just as strong a deterrent as prohibition, is not an appealing line of argument. The revenue goals for a legalized marijuana market should be moderate, meaning no more extreme (relative to price) than those for alcohol or tobacco.

A second caveat is that although marijuana is more commonly used than other drugs, prohibition targets other drugs disproportionately relative to marijuana. Thus, at least from the perspective of saving enforcement resources, it is misguided to think only about legalizing marijuana. The same caveat potentially applies if the focus is raising tax revenue, since the demands for some other drugs are plausibly less responsive to price than is marijuana. This means policy can raise substantial revenue from these drugs even if the markets are smaller. Plausibly, the budgetary impacts from these other drugs would be several times larger than those from legalizing marijuana, even though they constitute a much smaller share of the market in terms of users.

An important clarification is that the tax revenues that would accrue to governments from legalization are not as cost-saving in the economic, "opportunity" sense of costs. Instead, these amounts represent transfers from those paying the tax (marijuana producers and users) to the general public. Under prohibition no taxation occurs, but consumers pay higher prices to producers. Thus, the distributional consequence of legalization is to redistribute wealth from people who choose to violate the law—by producing and selling marijuana under prohibition—to the general public. This redistribution is one that most people would endorse, but it does not represent a net increase in resources.

One criticism of legalization proposals that highlight the increase in tax revenues asserts that the underground marijuana industry would remain underground even if legalized, thereby limiting the scope for taxing legalized marijuana. This concern has a grain of truth but is almost certainly irrelevant in practice. Home production of alcohol was widespread during Prohibition, but after repeal most of the demand reverted to being met by commercial suppliers. This makes sense, since large-scale, commercial production is more efficient, and most people seem to prefer purchasing from a reliable, long-term supplier who can maintain quality and consistency. (Most people could grow their own tomatoes, but only a tiny fraction of the population chooses to do so.)

The Broader Issues Related to Marijuana Legalization

The budgetary impacts of marijuana legalization are not trivial. A savings of $7.7 billion per year in resources is substantial, and a net improvement in the U.S. government budget of $10–14 billion annually is worth achieving. Compared

---

Reduced Government Expenditure Due to Marijuana Legalization, in Billions of Dollars

	State and local	Federal	Total
Arrests	$1.8		
Prosecutions	$3.2		
Incarcerations	$0.5		
Total	$5.5	$2.5	$8.0

TAKEN FROM: Jeffrey Miron, "A Cost-Benefit Analysis of Legalizing Marijuana," *The Pot Book: A Complete Guide to Cannabis: Its Role in Medicine, Politics, Science, and Culture,* edited by Julie Holland. Rochester, VT: Park Street Press, 2010.

---

to the size of the U.S. economy or government, however, these are not enormous amounts. Thus, if prohibition has some nontrivial benefit and few unintended negatives, prohibition advocates could rationally argue that the budgetary benefits do not justify legalization. It is crucial, therefore, to consider the broader range of issues involved. In fact, prohibition has minimal benefits and substantial negative side effects beyond its direct costs.

Prohibition does not eliminate the market for marijuana. Instead, prohibition creates a black market. The key question for analysis of prohibition versus legalization is therefore to what degree marijuana use in this black market is less than what would occur under legalization. To address this issue, consider the effects of prohibition on the demand for and supply of marijuana.

Prohibition affects the demand for marijuana in several ways. The mere existence of prohibition might reduce demand if some consumers exhibit respect for the law. The evidence suggests, however, that "respect for the law" exerts only a mild effect, since violation of weakly enforced laws (speeding, tax evasion, blue laws, sodomy laws) is widespread. The penalties for marijuana purchase or possession might reduce demand by raising the effective price of marijuana use. Again, however, the evidence does not suggest a major impact given that most such penalties are mild and rarely imposed. Potentially countering any tendency for prohibition to reduce demand, prohibition might increase demand because it makes marijuana a "forbidden fruit." Prohibition also affects the supply of marijuana. Because black market marijuana suppliers must operate in secret and attempt to avoid detection by law enforcement, they face increased costs of manufacturing, transporting, and distributing marijuana. Conditional on operating in secret, however, black market suppliers face low marginal costs of evading tax laws and regulatory policies, and this partially offsets the increased costs of operating secretly. Other differences between a black market and a legal market (e.g., differences in advertising incentives or market power) have ambiguous implications for supply costs under prohibition versus legalization.

The bottom line is that prohibition probably reduces marijuana use, since the direct effects on both supply and demand suggest this outcome. Theory does not dictate that prohibition causes a large reduction in marijuana use, however, and the evidence suggests prohibition has at most a moderate impact. Alcohol prohibition in the United States, for example, did not appear to have reduced alcohol consumption dramatically. Comparisons of countries with weakly versus strongly imposed prohibitions find little evidence of higher marijuana consumption in the weak enforcement countries. Thus the evidence does not rule out the possibility that marijuana consumption might increase, say, 25 percent under legalization, but no evidence suggests it would be increased by orders of magnitude.

Effects of Prohibition

Whatever the impact of prohibition on marijuana consumption, prohibition has numerous effects beyond any direct costs of enforcement. The main ones are as follows:

Increased crime and corruption. Because participants in illegal markets cannot resolve disputes with nonviolent mechanisms like courts and lawyers, they use guns instead; thus prohibition increases violent crime. By diverting criminal justice resources to prohibition enforcement, prohibition causes reduced deterrence of all kinds of crime. Because participants in a black market must either evade law enforcement authorities or pay them to look the other way, prohibition encourages corruption.

Harm to marijuana users. By raising prices and creating the threat of arrest and other legal sanctions, prohibition reduces the welfare of those who use marijuana illegally. These users also spend more time trying to buy marijuana and must deal with criminals to do so.

Reduced product quality. In a legal market, consumers who purchase faulty goods can punish suppliers by pursuing liability claims, by generating bad publicity, by avoiding repeat purchases, or by complaining to private or government watchdog groups. In a black market, these mechanisms for ensuring product quality are unavailable or less effective. This means product quality is lower and more uncertain in an underground market.

Enriching criminals. In a legal market, the income generated by production and sale of marijuana is subject to taxation, and the tax revenues accrue to the government. In a black market, suppliers capture these revenues as profits. Prohibition thus enriches the segment of society most willing to evade the law.

Restrictions on medicinal uses of marijuana. Because of prohibition, marijuana is even more tightly controlled than morphine or cocaine and cannot be used for medical purposes despite abundant evidence that it alleviates nausea, pain, and muscle spasms, as well as symptoms of glaucoma, epilepsy, multiple sclerosis, AIDS, and migraine headaches, among other ailments.

Compromised civil liberties. Because marijuana "crimes" involve voluntary exchange, enforcement relies on asset seizures, aggressive search tactics, and racial profiling. All these tactics strain accepted notions of civil liberties and generate racial tension.

Respect for the law. All experience to date indicates that, even with substantial enforcement, prohibition fails to deter a great many persons from supplying and consuming marijuana. This fact signals users and nonusers that "laws are for suckers"; prohibition therefore undermines the spirit of voluntary compliance that is essential to law enforcement in a free society.

Most effects of prohibition are unambiguously undesirable. The only possible exception is prohibition's impact in reducing marijuana consumption. According to some people, marijuana use is inherently evil, or promotes socially undesirable behavior, or lowers health and productivity, implying policy-induced reductions in marijuana use might be desirable.

The claim that marijuana is inherently wrong is simply an assertion devoid of any science or reason, however, and no valid evidence supports the claim that marijuana use causes poor health, diminished productivity, or other unwanted behaviors.

An alternative view is that marijuana consumption can generate negative side effects, such as traffic accidents. This view is defensible, but a better approach would be policies that target the negative behavior itself, namely laws against driving under the influence. This is exactly what current policy does regarding alcohol. A total prohibition on marijuana targets millions of otherwise law-abiding citizens whose use does not generate adverse effects for anyone.

Overall, therefore, the reduction in marijuana consumption caused by prohibition is a cost rather than a benefit. That is, preventing responsible people from consuming marijuana makes them worse off, just as preventing responsible people from consuming alcohol would make them worse off. This means virtually all of prohibition's consequences are undesirable, so it is impossible to justify any government expenditure in the attempt to implement this policy.

Many Costs of Prohibition

The government expenditure utilized in the attempt to enforce marijuana prohibition is an unambiguous cost of prohibition relative to legalization. It is far from the only cost, however. Prohibition has a host of unintended negative effects that should receive at least as much consideration in evaluations of marijuana policy.

Perhaps most importantly, prohibition reduces the welfare of people who can and do use marijuana with little harm to themselves or others and who believe they receive a benefit—whether recreational or medicinal—from marijuana use. A policy that prohibits marijuana makes no more sense than a policy that prohibits alcohol, ice cream, or driving on the highway. Each of these activities—and millions of others—can generate harm when conducted irresponsibly but also has the potential to benefit the vast majority of users. This is a crucial effect of marijuana legalization that all analyses should recognize.

| *"As long as federal law proscribes marijuana ... a state tax on marijuana would be largely unsuccessful."*

Legalizing Marijuana in California Would Not Generate Substantial Tax Revenues

Robert A. Mikos

Robert A. Mikos is a professor of law at Vanderbilt University. In the following viewpoint, he argues that states are unlikely to solve their budget problems by taxing marijuana. He says that the federal ban on marijuana will make it extremely difficult for states to regulate or tax marijuana. He concludes that there may be good reasons to legalize marijuana, however, unless there is a change in federal law, generating revenue will not be one of them.

As you read, consider the following questions:

1. How much does California spend on marijuana prohibition, according to the viewpoint?

Robert A. Mikos, "State Taxation of Marijuana Distribution and Other Federal Crimes," *Vanderbilt Public Law Paper, Vanderbilt Law and Economics Paper, University of Chicago Legal Forum*, no. 10–05; 10–04; 222, February 9, 2010, pp. 221–225, 259–261. Copyright © 2010 by University of Chicago Legal Forum. All rights reserved. Reproduced by permission.

2. What does Mikos say is essential to curbing tax evasion?

3. According to Mikos, why would a state not be able to sell marijuana through licensed stores?

The financial crisis has breathed new life into proposals to reform marijuana law. Commentators suggest that legalizing and taxing marijuana could generate substantial revenues for beleaguered state governments—as much as $1.4 billion for California alone. This [viewpoint], however, suggests that commentators have grossly underestimated the difficulty of collecting a tax on a drug that remains illegal under federal law. The federal ban on marijuana will impair state tax collections for two reasons. First, by giving marijuana distributors powerful incentives to stay small and operate underground, the federal ban will make it difficult for states to monitor marijuana distribution and, consequently, to detect and deter tax evasion. In theory, states could bolster deterrence by increasing sanctions for tax evasion, but doing so seems politically infeasible and may not even work. Second, even if states could find a way to monitor marijuana distribution effectively (for example, by licensing distributors) such monitoring could backfire. Any information the states gather on marijuana distribution could be seized by federal authorities and used to impose federal sanctions on distributors, giving them added incentive to evade state tax authorities. For both reasons, a marijuana tax may not be the budget panacea proponents claim it would be. To be sure, there are reasonable arguments favoring legalization; rescuing states from dire fiscal straits, however, is not one of them.

Criminal Penalties and the Budget Crisis

Fighting crime is enormously expensive. Federal and state governments together spend more than $200 billion annually on criminal justice. Over the past few decades, these expenditures have ballooned due to the adoption of aggressive new anti-crime policies, including three strikes sentencing laws [that impose minimum sentences for repeat offenders] and expanded criminal liability. Some prominent legal scholars have suggested that the expansion in the scope and severity of the criminal law might never end—or at least, might never reverse itself—given the public's seemingly insatiable demand for retribution and safety.

Now, however, fiscal reality is casting doubt on that received wisdom. With some states teetering on the brink of financial ruin, lawmakers are starting to question whether tough crime-fighting measures are really worth their costs. Searching for ways to cut criminal justice expenditures, state lawmakers have proposed furloughing prisoners, switching to less costly forms of punishment, and trimming the ranks of police forces.

Even more interestingly, a few states have seriously contemplated legalizing activities long considered criminal, including the possession, cultivation, and distribution of marijuana. Though marijuana has long been a drain on state budgets—California alone reportedly spends $156 million annually combating the drug—some state lawmakers are beginning to see it as a panacea for state budget woes. They hope to ease the strain on their criminal justice budgets—and create a new stream of tax revenue—by legalizing and taxing distribution of the drug.

California, perhaps the most financially distraught of the states, has been leading the charge to legalize and tax marijuana. Several proposals now under consideration would make the cultivation, distribution, and possession of marijuana legal for adults. Proponents suggest the groundbreaking reforms could save California the estimated $156 million it currently spends investigating, arresting, prosecuting, and imprisoning recreational marijuana dealers and users. Even more impressively, by subjecting the drug to a special tax—a $50 levy for every ounce of marijuana sold—along with the sales tax that applies to all commodities, the proposal would generate an estimated $1.382 billion in new tax revenue for the beleaguered state. Given that Californians reportedly produce nearly $14 billion in marijuana each year—and consume much of that in-state—one can hardly blame lawmakers' enthusiasm for getting a cut of the action.

Indeed, lured by the promise of substantial tax revenues, nearly 700,000 Californians have signed petitions assuring that at least one proposal to legalize and tax marijuana (Proposition 19) will appear on the California ballot in 2010. The question is whether legislators and voters are buying a pig in a poke. [Editor's note: The California voters rejected Proposition 19 on November 2, 2010.]

Revenue Is Overestimated

This [viewpoint] suggests that proponents have grossly overestimated the marijuana tax's revenue potential by downplaying, or simply ignoring, the complexities of enforcing it. In general, tax proponents and many commentators have assumed the states could collect a marijuana tax as easily as they collect taxes on other "sins," such as cigarettes, without grappling with the unique issues posed by the federal ban. Opponents, by contrast, have assumed that distributors would necessarily evade the marijuana tax, without explaining why marijuana tax collections would fare *worse* than taxes imposed on other sins—a particularly egregious omission given that many extant sin taxes exceed the proposed marijuana tax. On all sides of the debate, commentary largely ignores—or makes undeveloped assumptions about—the role that federal law would play in state tax collections. Those commentators who have paid heed to the federal ban seem to agree that federal law poses a barrier to a state marijuana tax, but no one has explained in any depth how or why this is the case.

This [viewpoint] seeks to fill that analytical void by analyzing the incentives to evade a state marijuana tax, in light of the enforcement mechanisms proposed by the state and the

Marijuana Revenues Are Uncertain

Our analysis reveals that projections about the impact of legalizing marijuana in California on consumption and public budgets are subject to considerable uncertainty. Although the state could see large increases in consumption and substantial positive budget effects, it could also see increases in consumption and low revenues due to tax evasion or a "race to the bottom" in terms of local tax rates.

Decision makers should view skeptically any projections that claim either precision or accuracy. In particular, we highlight two distinct drivers of uncertainty that surround these estimates of consumption and tax revenues: uncertainty about parameters (such as how legalization will affect production costs and price) and uncertainty about structural assumptions (such as the federal response to a state that allows production and distribution of a substance that would still be illegal under federal law). Such uncertainties are so large that altering just a few key assumptions or parameter values can dramatically change the results.

Beau Kilmer et al., Altered State?: Assessing How Marijuana Legalization in California Could Influence Marijuana Consumption and Public Budgets. *Santa Monica, CA: RAND Corporation, 2010.*

ignored or misunderstood wrench thrown into the machine by federal law. It starts with the standard economic model of tax evasion employed in the tax compliance literature. According to that literature, collecting reliable information on taxable activity is essential to curbing tax evasion. In a nutshell, to stop distributors from evading the marijuana tax, states must gather detailed information on their sales; the more information the states gather, the stronger will be distributors' incentives to pay. The fragmentation of the marijuana market, however, threatens to overwhelm state monitoring of distribution. Thousands of suppliers now compete in the marijuana market, and the continuing federal ban will thwart consolidation even if California (or any other state) legalizes marijuana.

What is more, measures that might otherwise facilitate monitoring of a fragmented marijuana distribution system (for example, a distributor licensing system) could easily backfire, since distribution remains a crime under federal law. States cannot necessarily block federal authorities from seizing the information they glean from drug distributors. In many cases, federal law enforcement officials could use this information to track down and sanction tax-abiding distributors. The risk that federal authorities could seize data collected by the states gives distributors added incentive, besides the tax, to evade state detection. . . .

Federal Law Will Undermine State Revenue

This [viewpoint] has examined a proposed state marijuana tax to highlight previously ignored tax compliance problems states face when attempting to tax goods or services that are forbidden under federal law. Due largely to the strains caused by the recession and attendant fiscal crises, several states are seriously contemplating legalizing and taxing marijuana. The financial allure is enormous—policy makers and economists suggest that a marijuana tax could generate billions in new revenues for the states.

The federal ban on marijuana, however, complicates enforcement of the tax. In particular, the federal ban makes state monitoring of marijuana distribution especially difficult and potentially self-defeating. First, the federal ban will keep the marijuana market fragmented. This means that thousands of small growers and distributors will continue to compete on the marijuana market, potentially overwhelming limited state tax collection resources. Second, even assuming a state could find a way to track taxable marijuana sales, doing so would only create a new problem. Federal law enforcement agents could use this state-gathered information to impose harsh federal sanctions on tax-paying marijuana distributors. The threat of being exposed in state records gives marijuana distributors an additional incentive—above and beyond the state tax—to evade state tax authorities. For both reasons, the continuing federal ban on marijuana is likely to exacerbate a marijuana tax gap. The states might collect only a fraction of the revenues proponents now claim a tax would generate.

There is no obvious solution to the problems posed by the federal ban, short of federal legalization. Many of the steps states could normally take to enhance tax compliance would be stymied or preempted by federal law. A state, for example, could not sell marijuana at state-operated stores; this option is clearly preempted by the CSA [Controlled Substances Act], which bars states—no less than private citizens—from distributing the drug. A state could attempt to foster consolidation of the marijuana market—for example, by limiting the number of licenses it issues or by imposing a lower tax rate on larger distributors—but doing so would not relieve distributors' fears of getting caught in the crosshairs of federal prosecutors. Allowing distributors to pay the tax anonymously would eliminate the paper trail for federal authorities, but it seems unlikely to deter tax evasion—existing drug taxes are paid anonymously and generate paltry revenues. The most promising reform could be to focus on taxing medical marijuana. The federal government's announcement that it would halt enforcement of the federal ban on medical marijuana would seemingly pave the way for consolidation of this niche market and would remove the concern that federal agents would use state-gathered information against medical marijuana distributors. A tax on this niche market, however, would generate only a fraction of the revenues now being touted by tax proponents. What is more, singling out medical marijuana for taxation could prove politically unpalatable; indeed, many state lawmakers are considering exempting medical marijuana from any marijuana tax.

In sum, as long as federal law proscribes marijuana—and federal agents remain committed to enforcing the ban—a state tax on marijuana would be largely unsuccessful. The tax would not force marijuana users to internalize the social costs of their activity; nor would it be a panacea for state budget woes. There are reasonable arguments favoring legalization of marijuana; rescuing the states from dire fiscal straits, however, is not one of them.

> *"Before Mexico's current war on drugs started, in late 2006, the country's crime rate was low and dropping."*

Legalizing Marijuana Will Reduce Drug Violence in Mexico

Héctor Aguilar Camín and Jorge G. Castañeda

Héctor Aguilar Camín is a historian, a novelist, and the publisher and editor of the Mexican magazine Nexos; *Jorge G. Castañeda is a former foreign minister of Mexico. In the following viewpoint, the authors argue that the war on drugs has enacted an enormous cost on Mexico by funding drug cartels that have ramped up crime and killed innocents. They say that legalizing marijuana and other drugs would undercut the cartels. The authors theorize that legalization in California, with which Mexico has a huge amount of trade, would pave the way for legalization efforts in Mexico. In November 2010, two months after this viewpoint was originally published, California voters rejected the ballot proposal, known as Proposition 19, to legalize marijuana in their state.*

As you read, consider the following questions:

1. What specific costs to Mexico do the authors attribute to the war on drugs?

2. In what way do the authors say the legalization debate is framed in Mexico?

3. According to the authors, why is drug abuse not a pressing problem in Mexico?

On Nov. 2 [2010], Californians will vote on Proposition 19, deciding whether to legalize the production, sale and consumption of marijuana. If the initiative passes, it won't just be momentous for California; it may, at long last, offer Mexico the promise of an exit from our costly war on drugs.

Mexico's Deadly Drug War

The costs of that war have long since reached intolerable levels: more than 28,000 of our fellow citizens dead since late 2006; expenditures well above $10 billion; terrible damage to Mexico's image abroad; human rights violations by government security forces; and ever more crime. In a recent poll by the Mexico City daily *Reforma*, 67 percent of Mexicans said these costs are unacceptable, while 59 percent said the drug cartels are winning the war.

We have believed for some time that Mexico should legalize marijuana and perhaps other drugs. But until now, most discussion of this possibility has foundered because our country's drug problem and the U.S. drug problem are so inextricably linked: What our country produces, Americans consume. As a result, the debate over legalization has inevitably gotten hung up over whether Mexico should wait until the United States is willing and able to do the same.

Proposition 19 changes this calculation. For Mexico, California is almost the whole enchilada: Our overall trade with the largest state of the union is huge, an immense number of

Californians are of Mexican origin, and an enormous proportion of American visitors to Mexico come from California. Passage of Prop 19 would therefore flip the terms of the debate about drug policy: If California legalizes marijuana, will it be viable for our country to continue hunting down drug lords in Tijuana? Will Wild West–style shootouts to stop Mexican cannabis from crossing the border make any sense when, just over that border, the local 7-Eleven sells pot?

The prospect of California legalizing marijuana coincides with an increasingly animated debate about legalization in Mexico. This summer [in 2010], our magazine, *Nexos*, asked the six leading [Mexican] presidential candidates whether, if California legalizes marijuana, Mexico should follow suit. Four of them said it should, albeit with qualifications. And last month, at a public forum presided over by President Felipe Calderón, one of us asked whether the time had come for such discussion to be taken seriously. Calderón's reply was startlingly open-minded and encouraging: "It's a fundamental debate," he said. ". . . You have to analyze carefully the pros and cons and the key arguments on both sides." The remarks attracted so much attention that, later in the day, Calderón backtracked, insisting that he was vehemently opposed to any form of legalization. Still, his comments helped stimulate the national conversation.

Mexico and Legalization

A growing number of distinguished Mexicans from all walks of life have recently come out in favor of some form of drug legalization. Former presidents Ernesto Zedillo and Vicente Fox, novelists Carlos Fuentes and Ángeles Mastretta, Nobel Prize–winning chemist Mario Molina, and movie star Gael García Bernal have all expressed support for this idea, and polls show that ordinary Mexicans are increasingly willing to contemplate the notion.

Indeed, as we have crisscrossed Mexico over the past six months on a book tour, visiting more than two dozen state capitals, holding town hall meetings with students, business-people, school teachers, local politicians and journalists, we have witnessed a striking shift in views on the matter. This is no longer your mother's Mexico—conservative, Catholic, introverted. Whenever we asked whether drugs should be legalized, the response was almost always overwhelmingly in favor of decriminalizing at least marijuana.

The debate here is not framed in terms of personal drug use but rather whether legalization would do anything to abate Mexico's nightmarish violence and crime. There are reasons to think that it would: The White House Office of National Drug Control Policy has said that up to 60 percent of Mexican drug cartels' profits come from marijuana. While some say the real figure is lower, pot is without question a crucial part of their business. Legalization would make a significant chunk of that business vanish. As their immense profits shrank, the drug kingpins would be deprived of the almost unlimited money they now use to fund recruitment, arms purchases and bribes.

In addition, legalizing marijuana would free up both human and financial resources for Mexico to push back against the scourges that are often, if not always correctly, attributed to drug traffickers and that constitute Mexicans' real bane: kidnapping, extortion, vehicle theft, home assaults, highway robbery and gunfights between gangs that leave far too many innocent bystanders dead and wounded. Before Mexico's current war on drugs started, in late 2006, the country's crime rate was low and dropping. Freed from the demands of the war on drugs, Mexico could return its energies to again reducing violent crime.

Marijuana as a First Step

Today, almost anyone caught carrying any drug in Mexico is subject to arrest, prosecution and jail. Would changing that increase consumption in Mexico? Perhaps for a while. Then again, given the extremely low levels of drug use in our country, the threat of drug abuse seems a less-than-pressing problem: According to a national survey in 2008, only 6 percent of Mexicans have ever tried a drug, compared with 47 percent of Americans, as shown by a different survey that year.

Still, real questions remain. Should our country legalize all drugs, or just marijuana? Can we legalize by ourselves, or does such a move make sense only if conducted hand in hand with the United States? Theoretically, the arguments in favor of marijuana legalization apply to virtually all drugs. We believe that the benefits would also apply to powder cocaine (not produced in Mexico, but shipped through our country en route from Latin America to the United States), heroin (produced in Mexico from poppies grown in the mountains of Sinaloa, Chihuahua and Durango) and methamphetamines (made locally with pseudoephedrine imported from China).

This is the real world, though, so we must think in terms of incremental change. It strikes us as easier and wiser to proceed step-by-step toward broad legalization, starting with marijuana, moving on to heroin (a minor trade in Mexico, and a manageable one stateside) and dealing only later, when Washington and others are ready, with cocaine and synthetic drugs.

For now we'll take California's ballot measure. If our neighbors to the north pass Proposition 19, our government will have two new options: to proceed unilaterally with legalization—with California but without Washington—or to hold off, while exploiting California's move to more actively lobby the U.S. government for wider changes in drug policy. Either way, the initiative's passage will enhance Calderón's moral authority in pressing [U.S.] President [Barack] Obama.

Our president will be able to say to yours: "We have paid an enormous price for a war that a majority of the citizens of your most populous and trend-setting state reject. Why don't we work together, producer and consumer nations alike, to draw a road map leading us away from the equivalent of Prohibition, before we all regret our shortsightedness?"

"There is no quick, politically feasible fix to reducing the DTO [drug trafficking organization] violence in Mexico."

Legalizing Marijuana in California Will Not Have Much Effect on Mexican Drug Traffickers

Beau Kilmer, Jonathan P. Caulkins, Brittany M. Bond, and Peter H. Reuter

Beau Kilmer, Jonathan P. Caulkins, Brittany M. Bond, and Peter H. Reuter are all researchers at the RAND Corporation. In the following viewpoint, they argue that legalizing marijuana in California will probably not have a major effect on drug violence in Mexico. They note that Mexican drug cartels get much less of their revenue from marijuana than is usually estimated and that California consumes only a fraction of the marijuana in the United States. The authors conclude that there is no quick fix for drug violence in Mexico.

As you read, consider the following questions:

1. What do the authors say are the security implications for the United States of rampant Mexican drug violence?

2. According to the authors, how much of Mexican DTO export revenue comes from marijuana, and how does this differ from widely cited figures?

3. What is the only way that legalizing marijuana in California could importantly cut DTO drug export revenue?

The recent [2010] surge in violence in Mexico has been dramatic. While the per capita murder rate fell by roughly 25 percent between 2000 and 2007, it jumped 50 percent between 2007 and 2009. The violence associated with the illicit drug trade is largely responsible for this reversal. The estimated annual total for drug-related homicides in Mexico increased from 1,776 in 2005 to 6,587 in 2009, and, in 2010, the total was already 5,775 by July [2010]. In 2009, the murder rate for drug-related homicides alone in Mexico exceeded the rate for all murders and nonnegligent manslaughters in the United States (6.1 versus 5.1 per 100,000).

Demand for Drugs and Violence

This violence in Mexico has security implications for the United States. The primary problem to date has *not* been violence spilling over the border. While there have been such incidents, and some are quite horrific, homicide rates in the U.S. cities along the Mexican border remain very low. El Paso is the second-safest city in the United States, with just 2.8 homicides per 100,000—a rate that is lower than that of Paris or Geneva. This is in sharp contrast to El Paso's twin city in Mexico, Ciudad Juárez, which experienced 2,754 homicides in 2009 (a rate of 196.7 per 100,000). While spillover violence does have important security implications for those living and working north of the border, this threat might have been exaggerated and pales in comparison to the lawlessness that pervades parts of Mexico. The bigger security implication for the United States is having a close ally and a large trading partner engulfed in such turmoil.

Demand for illicit drugs in the United States creates lucrative markets for the Mexican drug trafficking organizations (DTOs). Secretary of State Hillary Clinton, echoing President George W. Bush in 2001, noted that America's demand for drugs was a root cause of the violence. While this has led some to argue that priority should be given to reducing U.S. drug demand, [Peter H.] Reuter's assessment of the literature leads him to soberly conclude that "there is little that the U.S. can do to reduce consumption over the next five years that will help Mexico." This does not mean that a serious investment in reducing consumption among heavy users (especially those in criminal justice settings) is not good policy. It just means that one should not expect rapid results. The great bulk of drug demand comes from the minority of individuals who are the heavy users; reducing their consumption is difficult.

Legalizing drugs has been suggested as a quicker and more decisive solution to the violence. Most notably, former Mexican president Vicente Fox recently called for Mexico to legalize the production, distribution, and sale of all drugs as a way of reducing the DTOs' power and related violence. He advocated it "as a strategy to weaken and break the economic system that allows cartels to earn huge profits". Mexico's current president, Felipe Calderón, does not support legalization, but he has said that legalization should be a topic of discussion.

The consequences of Mexico unilaterally legalizing drug production and distribution are fairly easy to foresee. Legalization would limit DTO revenues from drug distribution in Mexico to revenues only derived from evading any associated taxes and regulations. However, unless the United States followed suit, Mexican DTOs would continue to profit by illegally smuggling drugs across the border. Comprehensive data on DTOs' full portfolio of revenues are understandably scarce, but no one believes that distribution to Mexican users is the primary revenue generator for DTOs.

Legalization in the United States

Not surprisingly, violence in Mexico plays a prominent role in debates about marijuana legalization in the United States. Often, big numbers of dubious origin are tossed around in drug policy discussions with little thought and, frankly, little consequence. Some U.S. government reports suggest that Mexican and Colombian DTOs combined earn $18 billion–$39 billion annually in wholesale drug proceeds, and one analysis even estimated that 60 percent of all Mexican DTO drug revenue comes from exporting marijuana. Legalization advocates seize on such figures to supplement their traditional arguments, and the figures have been repeated in the popular press, with even respectable news sources claiming that "the Mexican cartels could be selling $20 billion worth of marijuana in the U.S. market each year."

The $20 billion figure appears to come from multiplying a $525-per-pound markup by an estimate from the Mexican government that 35 million pounds were produced in Mexico and then rounding up. However, no data support the claim that U.S. users consume 35 million pounds (˜16,000 metric tons [MT]) per year, let alone that they consume this much marijuana from Mexico. This is *three* times the United Nations Office on Drugs and Crime's upper bound for total U.S. consumption and nearly *four* times the amount estimated by the Drug Enforcement Administration (DEA).

Nevertheless, the wide acceptance of such large numbers may have substantial consequences. In November 2010, California voters will decide on Proposition 19 (also known as the Regulate, Control and Tax Cannabis Act of 2010, or Prop 19). Proposition 19 would legalize marijuana possession for those

21 and older, permit adults to cultivate 5-foot-by-5-foot plots in their homes, and allow each local jurisdiction to enable, regulate, and tax commercial production and distribution. Advocates have argued that legalizing marijuana in California will reduce the role the Mexican DTOs play in supplying marijuana, thereby reducing violence. In particular, the official ballot argument for Proposition 19 states that "[m]arijuana prohibition has created vicious drug cartels across our border," and a proponent's website claims that Proposition 19 will "[c]ut off funding to violent drug cartels across our border who currently generate 60 percent of their revenue from the illegal U.S. marijuana market." [Editor's note: California voters rejected the proposal on November 2, 2010.]

Legalization May Not Help

This [viewpoint] seeks to provide a better understanding of how marijuana legalization in California could influence DTO revenues and the violence in Mexico. We focus on gross revenues from export and distribution to wholesale markets near the southwestern U.S. border. DTOs also generate revenue from operations further down the distribution chain in the United States. It is difficult to assess how much they make from such domestic (U.S.) distribution, and it is unclear how this would change post-legalization because distribution would become legal only for one drug in one state. The analysis is rooted in RAND's earlier report on marijuana legalization and provides a number of important, albeit preliminary, insights about the markets for cocaine, heroin, and methamphetamine. . . .

Our analysis leads to the following insights:

- Mexican DTOs' gross revenues from moving marijuana across the border into the United States and selling it to wholesalers is likely less than $2 billion, and our preferred estimate is closer to $1.5 billion. This figure does not include revenue from DTO production and distribution in the United States, which is extremely difficult to estimate with existing data.

- The ubiquitous claim that 60 percent of Mexican DTO export revenues come from U.S. marijuana consumption should not be taken seriously. No publicly available source verifies or explains this figure and subsequent analyses revealed great uncertainty about the estimate. Our analysis—though preliminary on this point—suggests that 15–26 percent is a more credible range of the share of drug export revenues attributable to marijuana.

- California accounts for about one-seventh of U.S. marijuana consumption, and domestic production is already stronger in California than elsewhere in the United States. Hence, if Prop 19 *only* affects revenues from supplying marijuana to California, DTO drug export revenue losses would be very small, on the order of 2–4 percent.

- The only way Prop 19 could importantly cut DTO drug *export* revenues is if California-produced marijuana is smuggled to other states at prices that outcompete current Mexican supplies. The extent of such smuggling will depend on a number of factors, including the actions of the federal government and other states. It is very hard to anticipate how the conflict between state, federal, and international law engendered by Prop 19 would play out, but it is important to note that hopes for substantially undermining DTO revenues are contingent on varying scenarios concerning that conflict.

- *If* marijuana can be diverted from legal production in California to other states and *if* smuggling it is no harder than it is to do today within U.S. borders, *then* California production could undercut sales of Mexican marijuana throughout much of the United States, cutting DTOs' marijuana export revenues by more than 65 percent and probably by 85 percent or more. However, there is significant uncertainty regarding the assumptions underlying this estimate, including (1) whether taxes are collected on the marijuana before it is diverted out of California's legal distribution chain, (2) how intense federal, state, and local enforcement efforts will be against that diverted marijuana, and (3) how many grams of lower-potency Mexican marijuana consumers will see as being equivalent to one gram of higher-potency, California-grown sinsemilla (i.e., how closely users view the two forms of the drug as substitutes).

• It is unclear whether reductions in Mexican DTOs' revenues from exporting marijuana would lead to corresponding decreases in violence. Some mechanisms suggest that large reductions in revenues could increase violence in the short run but decrease it in the long run.

• Drug markets are intrinsically difficult to measure, and estimates will never be precise. However, some of the current uncertainty stems from parameters that are not hard to study, such as the weight of an average marijuana joint. That the best nationally representative data on something so simple is almost 20 years old and is calculated indirectly reflects how disconnected data-collection agencies are from the policy process, and vice versa.

No Quick Fix

With respect to whether marijuana legalization in California could help reduce the violence in Mexico, our best answer is "not to any appreciable extent unless California exports drive

Mexican marijuana out of the market in other states; if that happens, in the long run, possibly yes, but unlikely much in the short run." There is no quick, politically feasible fix to reducing the DTO violence in Mexico. As a number of other researchers have noted, there are fundamental issues related to the justice system that need to be addressed before anyone can expect significant improvements in the security situation in Mexico.

Periodical and Internet Sources Bibliography

The following articles have been selected to supplement the diverse views presented in this chapter.

Randal C. Archibold   "Mexico Watches California Marijuana Vote," *New York Times*, October 17, 2010.

Jason Beaubien   "Cash from Marijuana Fuels Mexico's Drug War," NPR, May 19, 2010. www.npr.org.

Christian Science Monitor   "Benefits from a Marijuana Tax? California Is Dreaming," April 8, 2010.

Robert L. DuPont   "Why We Should Not Legalize Marijuana," CNBC, April 20, 2010. www.cnbc.com.

John Dyer   "A Budget Cure: Marijuana Taxes?," *MSN Money*, April 30, 2009. http://articles.money central.msn.com.

Los Angeles Times   "Study of Marijuana Tax Gets Support in Senate Committee," May 4, 2011.

Josh Marshall   "What Happened to Prop 19," *Talking Points Memo*, November 5, 2010. http://talkingpoints memo.com.

Scientific American   "Half-Baked Idea?: Legalizing Marijuana Will Help the Environment," May 20, 2011.

Andrew Sullivan   "Josh Marshall and the Weed," *The Atlantic*, November 5, 2010. www.theatlantic.com.

Lauren Villagran   "Marijuana Legalization in Mexico Gaining Support," *Dallas Morning News*, August 10, 2010.

For Further Discussion

Chapter 1

1. Rita Rubin argues that marijuana is a highly addictive drug that leads to the use of other illegal substances, while Bruce Mirken insists that marijuana is not a gateway drug. Based on your reading, do you believe that marijuana use leads an individual to try harder drugs such as cocaine or heroin? Explain your reasoning.

2. If marijuana is dangerous, does it follow that it should be illegal? Based on your reading in this chapter, do you think all potentially harmful substances should be outlawed? Explain your reasoning.

Chapter 2

1. Marie Myung-Ok Lee is a mother with an autistic child; Ugo Uche is a professional counselor. Based on their backgrounds and their viewpoints, who do you think is better qualified to decide whether Lee's child should be treated for autism with marijuana? Explain your reasoning.

2. Based on the viewpoints by William Saletan and Lanny Swerdlow, is the "high" one gets from drugs a good thing, or is the "high" part of what is wrong with drugs? Should society regulate substances that make people too happy, regardless of other effects? Explain your reasoning.

Chapter 3

1. Do you agree with George F. Will that state medical marijuana laws undermine federal law? Should states defer to federal law even if, as Sydney Spiesel suggests, federal law is not based on good science? Should the law be respected

even if it is unwise or biased? Or does the scientific debate affect whether the law should be respected? Explain your reasoning.

2. What is the law on medical marijuana in your state (or country, if you live outside the United States)? Based on the viewpoints in this chapter, do you think your state should tighten or loosen restrictions on medical marijuana?

Chapter 4

1. Charles Stimson says that marijuana should not be legalized because, unlike alcohol, it has no known medicinal uses. Based on this chapter and the previous chapter, is this accurate? Does Stimson have other arguments for the outlawing of marijuana even if it does have medicinal properties?

2. Jeffrey Miron argues that marijuana should be legalized, regardless of whether it makes sense in monetary terms to do so. Does his support for marijuana legalization in principle call into question the objectivity of his cost-benefit analysis? Explain your reasoning.

3. Do you think that the authors throughout this book looked to evidence to determine their opinions about marijuana, or do you think their opinions about marijuana determined the evidence they cite? Give examples of specific authors to buttress your argument.

Organizations to Contact

The editors have compiled the following list of organizations concerned with the issues debated in this book. The descriptions are derived from materials provided by the organizations. All have publications or information available for interested readers. The list was compiled on the date of publication of the present volume; the information provided here may change. Be aware that many organizations take several weeks or longer to respond to inquiries, so allow as much time as possible.

American Council for Drug Education (ACDE)
164 West Seventy-Fourth Street, New York, NY   10023
(800) 488-3784 • fax: (212) 595-2553
e-mail: acde@phoenixhouse.org
website: www.acde.org

The American Council for Drug Education (ACDE) informs the public about the harmful effects of abusing drugs and alcohol. It gives the public access to scientifically based, compelling prevention programs and materials. ACDE has resources for parents, youths, educators, prevention professionals, employers, health care professionals, and other concerned community members who are working to help America's youths avoid the dangers of drug and alcohol abuse. It publishes brochures, books, and other materials, all available for order through its website.

Americans for Safe Access (ASA)
1322 Webster Street, Suite 402, Oakland, CA   94612
(510) 251-1856 • fax: (510) 251-2036
e-mail: info@safeaccessnow.org
website: www.safeaccessnow.org

Americans for Safe Access (ASA) is a national grassroots coalition working with local, state, and national legislators to protect the rights of patients and doctors to legally use marijuana for medical purposes. It provides legal training for lawyers and patients, medical information for doctors and patients, media support for court cases, activist training for grassroots organizers, and rapid response to law enforcement encounters. ASA sends out *Weekly News Summaries* to update its members on legal cases and current events pertaining to marijuana.

Common Sense for Drug Policy

1377-C Spencer Avenue, Lancaster, PA   17603
(717) 299-0600 • fax: (717) 393-4953
e-mail: info@csdp.org
website: www.csdp.org

Common Sense for Drug Policy is a nonprofit organization dedicated to expanding discussion on drug policy by voicing questions about existing law and educating the public about alternatives to current policies. It offers advice and technical assistance to individuals and organizations working to reform current policies, hosts public forums, and provides pro bono legal assistance to those adversely affected by drug policy. It makes available numerous news articles, links, fact sheets, and publications, including *Drug War Facts*, on its website.

Marijuana Policy Project (MPP)

236 Massachusetts Avenue NE, Suite 400
Washington, DC   20002
(202) 462-5747
e-mail: info@mpp.org
website: www.mpp.org

The Marijuana Policy Project (MPP) develops and promotes policies to minimize the harm associated with marijuana laws. The project increases public awareness through speaking engagements, educational seminars, and the mass media. Briefing papers, news articles, op-eds, and reports are available on its website.

National Center on Addiction and Substance Abuse (CASA)
633 Third Avenue, 19th Floor, New York, NY 10017-6706
(212) 841-5200
website: www.casacolumbia.org

National Center on Addiction and Substance Abuse (CASA) is a private nonprofit organization that works to educate the public about the hazards of chemical dependency. The organization supports treatment as the best way to reduce chemical dependency. It produces numerous publications describing the harmful effects of alcohol and drug addiction and effective ways to address the problem of substance abuse. It publishes books such as *How to Raise a Drug-Free Kid* and reports, papers, and newsletters, which are available through its website.

National Institute on Drug Abuse (NIDA)
6001 Executive Boulevard, Room 5213
Bethesda, MD 20892-9561
(301) 443-1124
e-mail: information@nida.nih.gov
website: www.nida.nih.gov

The National Institute on Drug Abuse (NIDA) supports and conducts research on drug abuse to improve addiction prevention, treatment, and policy efforts. It is dedicated to understanding how commonly abused drugs affect the brain and behavior, and it works to rapidly disseminate new information to policy makers, drug abuse practitioners, other health care practitioners, and the general public. It prints the bimonthly *NIDA Notes* newsletter; *NIDA Capsules* fact sheets; and a catalog of research reports and public education materials, such as *Marijuana: Facts for Teens* and *Drugs, Brains, and Behavior: The Science of Addiction*.

National Organization for the Reform of Marijuana Laws (NORML)
1600 K Street NW, Mezzanine Level
Washington, DC 20006-2832
(202) 483-5500 • fax: (202) 483-0057

e-mail: norml@norml.org
website: www.norml.org

The National Organization for the Reform of Marijuana Laws
(NORML) fights to legalize marijuana and to help those who
have been convicted or sentenced for possessing or selling
marijuana. It asserts that marijuana can, and should, be used
responsibly by adults who so choose. NORML's website includes pamphlets, position papers, blogs, and news reports.

The Partnership at Drugfree.org
352 Park Avenue South, 9th Floor, New York, NY   10010
(212) 922-1560 • fax: (212) 922-1570
website: www.drugfree.org

Formerly known as the Partnership for a Drug-Free America,
the Partnership at Drugfree.org is a nonprofit organization
that utilizes the media to reduce demand for illicit drugs in
America. Best known for its national antidrug advertising
campaign, the partnership works to educate children about
the dangers of drugs and prevent drug use among youths. It
produces the *Partnership Newsletter*, annual reports, and
monthly press releases about current events with which the
partnership is involved.

RAND Corporation
1776 Main Street, PO Box 2138
Santa Monica, CA   90407-2138
(310) 393-0411 • fax: (310) 393-4818
website: www.rand.org

The RAND Corporation is a research institution that seeks to
improve public policy through research and analysis. RAND's
Drug Policy Research Center disseminates information on the
costs, prevention, and treatment of alcohol and drug abuse
and on trends in drug-law enforcement. Its extensive list of
publications includes the research brief *How State Medical
Marijuana Laws Vary: A Comprehensive Review* and the book
*Legalizing Marijuana: Issues to Consider Before Reforming Cali-
fornia State Law*.

US Drug Enforcement Administration (DEA)
Mailstop: AES, 8701 Morrissette Drive, Springfield, VA   22152
(202) 307-1000
website: www.justice.gov/dea

The US Drug Enforcement Administration (DEA) is the federal agency charged with enforcing the nation's drug laws. The organization concentrates on stopping the smuggling and distribution of narcotics in the United States and abroad. It publishes *Microgram Journal* biannually, *Microgram Bulletins* monthly, and drug prevention booklets such as *Get It Straight* and *Speaking Out Against Drug Legalization*.

Bibliography of Books

Joanne Baum

The Truth About Pot: Ten Recovering Marijuana Users Share Their Personal Stories. Center City, MN: Hazelden, 1998.

Richard Glen Boire and Kevin Feeney

Medical Marijuana Law. Oakland, CA: Ronin Publishing, 2006.

Martin Booth

Cannabis: A History. New York: Picador, 2005.

Joseph A. Califano Jr.

High Society: How Substance Abuse Ravages America and What to Do About It. New York: PublicAffairs, 2007.

Howard Campbell

Drug War Zone: Frontline Dispatches from the Streets of El Paso and Juárez. Austin: University of Texas Press, 2009.

Mitch Earleywine

Understanding Marijuana: A New Look at the Scientific Evidence. New York: Oxford University Press, 2002.

Mitch Earleywine, ed.

Pot Politics: Marijuana and the Costs of Prohibition. New York: Oxford University Press, 2007.

John Geluardi

Cannabiz: The Explosive Rise of the Medical Marijuana Industry. Sausalito, CA: PoliPoint Press, 2010.

Rudolph J. Gerber   *Legalizing Marijuana: Drug Policy Reform and Prohibition Politics.* Westport, CT: Praeger, 2004.

Dale Gieringer, Ed Rosenthal, and Gregory T. Carter   *Marijuana Medical Handbook: Practical Guide to the Therapeutic Uses of Marijuana.* Oakland, CA: Quick American, 2008.

George W. Grayson   *Mexico: Narco-Violence and a Failed State?* New Brunswick, NJ: Transaction Publishers, 2010.

Dirk Hanson   *The Chemical Carousel: What Science Tells Us About Beating Addiction.* Charleston, SC: BookSurge Publishing, 2009.

James A. Inciardi   *War on Drugs IV: The Continuing Saga of the Mysteries and Miseries of Intoxication, Addiction, Crime, and Public Policy.* 4th ed. Boston, MA: Pearson/Allyn & Bacon, 2008.

James Inciardi and Karen McElrath, eds.   *The American Drug Scene: An Anthology.* 6th ed. New York: Oxford University Press, 2011.

Leslie L. Iversen   *The Science of Marijuana.* New York: Oxford University Press, 2008.

Sam Kamin and Christopher S. Morris   *The Impact of the Decriminalization and Legalization of Marijuana: An Immediate Look at the Cannabis Reform Movement.* Boston, MA: Aspatore Books, 2010.

Beau Kilmer et al. *Altered State?: Assessing How Marijuana Legalization in California Could Influence Marijuana Consumption and Public Budgets.* Santa Monica, CA: RAND Corporation, 2010.

James Langton *No Need for Weed: Understanding and Breaking Cannabis Dependency.* Coventry, England: Hindsight Publishing, 2008.

Charles F. Levinthal *Drugs, Society, and Criminal Justice.* 3rd ed. Boston, MA: Prentice Hall, 2012.

Mickey Martin, Ed Rosenthal, and Gregory T. Carter *Medical Marijuana 101: Everything They Told You Is Wrong.* Oakland, CA: Quick American, 2011.

John Nores Jr. and James A. Swan *War in the Woods: Combating Marijuana Cartels on America's Public Lands.* Guilford, CT: Lyons Press, 2010.

Trish Regan *Joint Ventures: Inside America's Almost Legal Marijuana Industry.* Hoboken, NJ: Wiley, 2011.

Robin Room} et al. *Cannabis Policy: Moving Beyond Stalemate.* New York: Oxford University Press, 2010.

Ed Rosenthal and Steve Kubby with S. Newhart *Why Marijuana Should Be Legal.* 2nd ed. New York: Thunder's Mouth Press, 2003.

Eric Schlosser

Reefer Madness: Sex, Drugs, and Cheap Labor in the American Black Market. Boston, MA: Houghton Mifflin, 2004.

Index